YOUR BRAIN'S NOT BROKeN

WORKBOOK

YOUR BRAIN'S NOT BROKeN

WORKBOOK

Strategies for Navigating Your Emotions
and Life with ADHD

TAMARA ROSIER, PhD

 Revell

a division of Baker Publishing Group
Grand Rapids, Michigan

© 2025 by Tamara Rosier

Published by Revell
a division of Baker Publishing Group
Grand Rapids, Michigan
RevellBooks.com

Printed in the United States of America

ISBN 978-0-8007-4600-1 (paperback)
ISBN 978-1-4934-4871-5 (ebook)

Portions of this text are taken from *Your Brain's Not Broken*, published by Revell, 2021.

Cover design by Laura Powell

Baker Publishing Group publications use paper produced from sustainable forestry practices and postconsumer waste whenever possible.

25 26 27 28 29 30 31   7 6 5 4 3 2 1

CONTENTS

INTRODUCTION

Your brain's not broken, but if you are like me, sometimes it seems hardwired to resist change. Personal growth and attaining goals require tackling problematic ADHD symptoms, a challenging task. Many of us know that our ADHD symptoms are getting in our way, but we are unsure where to begin. We are like thirty-year-old Bonnie, who recognizes the impact of issues such as procrastination on her career goals but struggles to overcome them. She knows she must produce a portfolio to interview for a new job. Still, something seemingly more urgent always seems to distract her.

Or maybe you are like some of my clients who feel hopeless and lost, having tried various strategies unsuccessfully. They also fear addressing their ADHD symptoms because they view their potential failure as evidence of personal shortcomings.

Our brains aren't broken. Those of us with ADHD possess remarkable adaptability and exhibit flexible thinking that transcends conventional norms. We are often capable of continuously adapting plans, debating both sides of an argument, and transforming an old pair of jeans into a chic carryall. When we embrace our unique qualities, we can navigate our ADHD landscape, making small decisions that alter the course of our days. While daily ADHD challenges persist, our focus is not on perfection but on continual growth and progress. Our mission isn't surviving the monotony of mundane tasks; we aspire to thrive emotionally, physically, and spiritually, elevating each day beyond mere task management.

Creating change in our lives is tricky, though. Think about how you feel regarding your ability to change or to create a new behavior pattern.

What has been your biggest emotional hurdle to addressing your ADHD patterns? Circle one from this list:

1. You think it will mean more work, which already sounds tedious and exhausting.
2. You are unsure how to address your symptoms or where to start. Your uncertainty keeps you stuck.
3. You fear failure. You've already tried so many things and failed that you don't have the emotional energy to try again.
4. You have serious doubts that anything will work. Life has taught you that you are just who you are and you can't change.

5. Other: _____

Instead of arguing with yourself about why your reasons for changing things are invalid, let's accept that you have a good reason for not wanting to address your ADHD symptoms. Perhaps it's even a part of yourself that wants to protect you. Look at the answer you circled and accept it without self-condemnation or loathing. Write a brief note to yourself acknowledging your trepidation to change, showing compassion, and reassuring yourself that you will be okay. My note would go like this:

Dear Tamara, I know that you are frustrated with yourself and doing this workbook seems like another thing you won't complete. That's reasonable because we have an imaginary hall of shame that we walk through, reminding us of our past failures. Let's try this and agree to be open to learning and hopeful about our future.

Your note to yourself:

Return to this note each time you use this workbook. It will remind you to be kind and patient with yourself as you think about how ADHD is affecting your life.

Now that we've addressed some apprehension you may have, let's turn our attention to why you picked up this workbook. A client of mine shared her reason for wanting to work on her ADHD symptoms this way: "ADHD is affecting a lot of my life. Although I like some of my ADHD tendencies that inspire my spontaneity and creativity, there are some symptoms that I need to look at because they aren't helping me. If I do this work, I can be an even better version of myself. Specifically, I want to be a better mom to my ADHD kids. I will be a better parent if I manage my emotions better."

What are your positive reasons for addressing your ADHD symptoms? Circle all that you agree with:

1. *I find myself standing at a crucial juncture in my life.* Significant life events have the power to act as agents of transformation. Milestones such as marriage, parenthood, health trials, or retirement can compel you to reassess your behaviors and decisions.

2. *I belong to an inspiring support group that encourages me to do this.* Being in a supportive family, community, or social circle promotes changes and is a powerful motivator.

3. *I am internally driven to tackle my ADHD.* Intrinsic sources of inspiration, driven by a commitment to health, self-discovery, and personal fulfillment, propel transformation.

4. *I am paying too much in "ADHD tax."* Spontaneous online shopping sprees when you get distracted while browsing, parking tickets that pile up when you forget to feed the meter, penalties for late payments, and broken phone screens all add to your ADHD tax. Financial benefits can incentivize positive change.

5. Other: _____

Look at all the reasons you circled. What are some positive emotions attached to them (e.g., hope, excitement, determination, gratitude)?

_____

_____

_____

_____

Do You Have a Growth Mindset?

As you use this workbook, you may become frustrated, wanting to go faster so that you can change. Perhaps you are sick and tired of your ADHD symptoms, and you want immediate relief. Nurturing a growth mindset will help you find the patience you need for yourself and the pace at which you complete this book.

A growth mindset is a psychological framework and attitude toward learning and development. Coined by psychologist Carol S. Dweck, the concept contrasts with a fixed mindset.[1] Individuals with a growth mindset believe their abilities and intelligence can be developed through dedication, hard work, learning, and perseverance. They see challenges as opportunities for learning and improvement. Instead of avoiding difficulties, they approach them positively, understanding that overcoming obstacles leads to personal growth.

Take an inventory of your growth mindset qualities. Circle which strengths you already have:

1. I embrace challenges.

2. I believe that putting in effort is crucial for becoming skilled at something new.

3. I learn from feedback and sometimes even criticism.

4. I persevere in the face of setbacks.

5. Instead of being envious of others' success, I am inspired by it.

6. I love learning. Even though it can be difficult, it's worth it.

7. I believe I can make improvements in my life.

8. I think focusing more on my steps rather than just the outcome is essential.

9. I celebrate my efforts, not just my achievements.

10. I am open to trying new strategies.

Now place an asterisk (*) next to the qualities you want to make even stronger.

When you're working on self-improvement, adopting a growth mindset is beneficial. Personal growth is a complex and winding road, not always straightforward. It evolves. It means taking apart what you know and compiling it with new information. This process may mean changing your mind (or your answers in this workbook) as you gain a deeper understanding. Reassure yourself that it is okay when you are frustrated by not having all the answers and feel uncertain. Accepting that you don't know everything allows new ideas to surface. Understanding the impact of

ADHD on your life, learning to manage emotions, and applying practical strategies to accomplish tasks are all part of this challenging but rewarding journey.

Bring a Friend Along

Have you considered working with a friend, spouse, family member, or coach as you complete this workbook? The social interaction inherent in working together can make this experience more enjoyable, reducing stress and fostering a positive attitude toward learning. In addition to promoting camaraderie and shared responsibility, working with someone else creates a supportive environment for tackling challenging exercises, reducing your feelings of overwhelm and frustration. Discussions with others about this workbook can lead to a deeper understanding of the material as different perspectives and approaches are brought to the table. This collaborative learning process enhances comprehension and helps you develop critical thinking and problem-solving skills.

About This Workbook

Each chapter in this workbook, designed to be used with my book *Your Brain's Not Broken*, consists of four key elements: Reflection on Reading, Questions and Exercises, Reinforcing Your Personal Growth, and Big Ideas. The Reflection on Reading section begins each chapter with questions designed to explore and discuss your personal response to the chapter's content. Digging into your interpretation assists in making connections and enhancing your understanding of your experiences with ADHD.

The Questions and Exercises section further builds on your perspective, encouraging the application of information from the book. If any exercise or question seems overwhelming, seek support to navigate your thoughts and feelings.

Reinforcing Your Personal Growth provides opportunities for reflecting on your developmental process, prompting you to recognize the strengths you bring.

Each chapter concludes with a Big Ideas box, where you can record key points to remember. As you read and learn, identify core concepts and main ideas, summarizing them in your own words to reinforce your memory. Regularly revisit these key concepts to enhance your short-term and long-term memory transfer.

Finally, embrace your curiosity, courage, and humility. Curiosity drives us to seek answers and learn, helping us to overcome the frustration of thinking and learning and to keep exploring. Remaining curious when faced with uncertainty allows us to trust that we'll figure things out eventually.

Courage prompts us to face the unknown and trust in the process of personal growth. Breaking down existing knowledge and rebuilding it with new insights is tough. Sitting with contradictions and accepting ambiguity is an intellectual bravery that allows new ideas to flourish.

Humility reminds us that we don't have all the answers. It encourages continuous learning and asking for feedback.

While I can't promise this workbook will eliminate unwanted behaviors and instill you with all you need to move forward, it can certainly guide you on a journey of self-discovery, helping you understand ADHD patterns and providing tools to address them. Though you may not solve your ADHD challenges today, you're building resources for your future self. Incorporating curiosity, courage, and humility sets the stage for ongoing personal growth.

Keep growing,
Tamara

1

And Then *Ping!* Goes My Brain

This first chapter explores the signs of ADHD, highlighting common indicators such as trouble directing and sustaining attention, hyperfocus, hyperactivity, impulsivity, and difficulty managing emotions. As you consider your symptoms, remain curious about them.

REFLECTION on READING

After reading this chapter,

I am feeling _____

_____

I am wondering _____

_____

I am wishing _____

_____

I want to learn more about _____

_____

What examples from Kristine's life in *Your Brain's Not Broken* resonated with you?

_____

_____

_____

_____

How are your experiences different from hers?

_____

_____

_____

_____

Questions and Exercises

Circle all the ADHD symptoms that you experience:

- Difficulty managing emotions
- Having a short attention span and being easily distracted
- Making careless mistakes
- Appearing forgetful or losing things
- Being unable to concentrate on tasks
- Being unable to stick to tasks that are tedious or time-consuming
- Appearing to be unable to listen to or carry out instructions
- Constantly changing activities or tasks
- Having difficulty organizing tasks

- Being unable to sit still, especially in calm or quiet surroundings
- Talking excessively
- Being unable to wait your turn
- Acting without thinking
- Interrupting conversations
- Other: _____
- Other: _____
- Other: _____
- Other: _____

Look at the symptoms you circled. Identify the top three that provide the most inconvenience for you. List them here and describe how they interfere with your life:

Symptom	Examples of how this interferes with your life	Examples of how this affects others in your life	Frequency of occurrence (daily, weekly, etc.)	How I feel about myself when this symptom occurs

REINFORCING
YOUR PERSONAL GROWTH

As I did these exercises, I demonstrated curiosity when I

As I did these exercises, I demonstrated courage when I

As I did these exercises, I demonstrated humility when I

BIG IDEAS
in Chapter 1

The metaphor we use to
describe our ADHD can help us
unlock how we address it.
It helps us name the parts of it.

Elves, Dirty Babies, and Lucille Ball

In this chapter, you will read examples of how individuals with ADHD use metaphors to gain insight into self-acceptance, perseverance, and solutions.

REFLECTION on READING

After reading this chapter,

I am feeling _____

_____

_____

_____

I am wondering _____

_____

_____

_____

I am wishing _____

_____

_____

_____

I want to learn more about _____

_____

_____

_____

I am frustrated that _____

_____

_____

_____

Questions and Exercises

This chapter describes the "simple tasks" that Claire finds difficult. List the seemingly simple tasks that you find difficult.

Task	Why it feels so difficult	How I feel about myself when I think about doing this task
Example: Managing my calendar	*Example:* There are so many moving parts that I feel overwhelmed.	*Example:* I feel stupid. Others can do this.

Do you see any patterns after completing this chart? What do the tasks have in common? What do your reasons for finding the tasks difficult have in common? Is there a pattern in how you feel about yourself?

_____

_____

_____

_____

Your Metaphor

I ask clients to create a metaphor—a word picture—of how they see their ADHD. Although there are themes and patterns to behavior, ADHD can present very differently from person to person, and metaphors help me understand those differences. I love the emails I've received from readers describing their metaphor. Some described their ADHD as an uncontrollable tornado that whips through anything they try to accomplish or as a monster lurking in the shadows.

Once you understand how you see your ADHD, you can begin to resolve the metaphor. Taking a holistic approach like this helps you see the big picture, identify what can be changed, and learn to problem-solve in real time.

How would you describe your ADHD? Take a moment to reflect on how you view this part of yourself, and create a word picture of it. It doesn't matter what your word picture is. You can use whatever metaphor works for you to get a better idea of how you view your ADHD and to change your perceptions of it strategically. In *Your Brain's Not Broken*, Claire looked out for distracting elves. Melanie decided to take care of her dirty baby. Kelly developed skills for managing the chocolates on the conveyor. Rick learned to put down his mask as he practiced a slower pace, allowing him to check in with his true thoughts and feelings before creating plans. And I have learned to have patience when trying to run a three-legged race.

Think imaginatively about what you're trying to describe. What characteristics does ADHD have? What does it do? How does it make you feel? Does it have a smell or taste? Does it remind you of an animal or an activity? Brainstorm by writing down whatever descriptions come to mind. Don't self-edit too heavily in this step; your goal is to generate a bunch of information to use. You can always scrap ideas that don't work later.

Draw or describe your metaphor:

Unpacking Your Metaphor

What about your metaphor hits home for you?

_____

_____

_____

What does your metaphor help you see or understand?

_____

_____

_____

What "problem" does your metaphor describe?

_____

_____

_____

After completing this exercise, what has become a little clearer about how you see your ADHD?

_____

_____

_____

REINFORCING
YOUR PERSONAL GROWTH

While completing this chapter, I used my growth mindset when

I am pleased with my metaphor because

I am going to remind myself about this metaphor by

When I noticed that I was frustrated while completing this chapter, I

I was patient with myself when

BIG IDEAS
in Chapter 2

3

The Case of the Missing Butler

This chapter explores how ADHD can lead to overwhelming emotional flooding in our brains, characterized by rapid shifts and heightened intensity. Instead of judging your emotions, remain curious about them as you use these questions to examine your experience.

REFLECTION on READING

What was the most memorable thing about this chapter?

_____

_____

_____

What did this chapter make you think about?

_____

_____

_____

How does this chapter connect with your experience?

_____

_____

_____

What do you want to know more about now? Why?

_____

_____

_____

Who do you wish would read this chapter? Why? What would reading it make them say, see, or do?

_____

_____

_____

Questions and Exercises

Like a Light Switch

Those of us with ADHD are often like a light switch when it comes to our emotions, motivations, and actions. When presented with a task, we will most likely respond with one of two settings or emotional responses: On (intense emotion—passionate, fixated, highly motivated) or Off (little or no emotion—disinterest or little motivation).

Describe the kinds of tasks you do when your light switch is Off.

_____

_____

_____

_____

Describe the kinds of tasks you do when your light switch is On.

_____

_____

_____

_____

Describe a time when you felt like you had a dimmer switch and were able to do something without great emotional effort.

_____

_____

_____

_____

Intense Emotions

Many times, individuals with ADHD feel strong emotions that appear extreme or exaggerated to others. Recent research reveals that those with ADHD can become significantly more frustrated, can lose their tempers more frequently, and are generally more excitable than non-ADHD individuals. The fluctuating and distorted emotional responses contribute extensively to challenges in home life, school, and work. For the most part, these big emotions are normal in every way except for their intensity.

The first step in managing intense emotions is to learn to see the bigness of them. Imagine placing the intensity of emotions along a continuum from 1 to 10, where 1 equals low or no feeling—almost apathy—and 10 equals intense feeling. Individuals without ADHD will spend most of their day in the center of the spectrum—at 4, 5, or 6—even though they have access to the full continuum.

1   2   3   **4**   **5**   **6**   **7**   **8**   **9**   **10**

Describe how your emotions look at a high intensity (9 or 10).

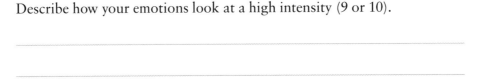

What types of situations bring you to a 9 or 10?

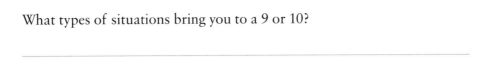

How do you return to a 4 or 5? Or do you go to a 1 or 2?

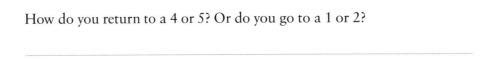

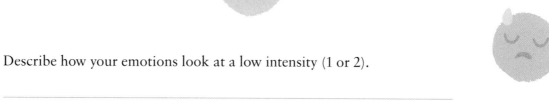

Describe how your emotions look at a low intensity (1 or 2).

_____

_____

_____

What types of situations bring you to a 1 or 2?

_____

_____

_____

How do you return to a 4 or 5? Or do you go to a 9 or 10?

_____

_____

_____

Plutchik's Wheel of Emotion is a visualization of the complexity of emotions and aids emotional identification. Use the Wheel of Emotion to help label your emotions and increase your self-awareness. Emotions farther from the center represent milder intensity. Emotions that are close to each other are more similar than those farther apart. The words outside of the petals are common blends of emotion. You can see a color version of Plutchik's Wheel of Emotion, figure 3.1, at the back of the book.

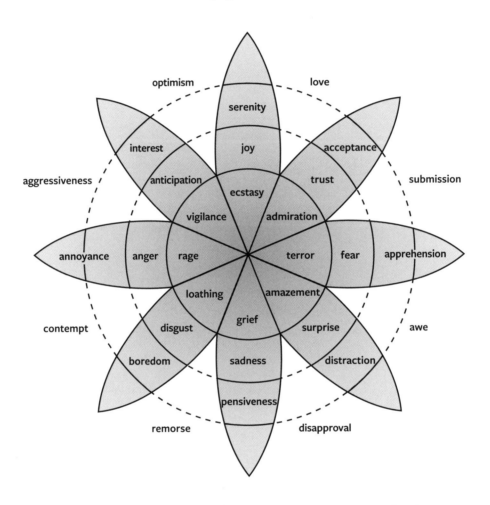

Think about the last time you had an intense emotion. Describe the situation.

_____

_____

Identify the primary emotion: Start by pinpointing on the wheel the primary emotion you were experiencing. Describe how the feeling grew.

_____

_____

Determine the intensity: Assess the intensity of the emotion you were feeling. If you were to attach a number from 1 to 10, what would it be?

Evaluate your triggers and context: Consider what triggered your emotion and the context in which it occurred. Understanding the circumstances that led to your emotional response can provide valuable insights into your emotional patterns and behaviors.

Assess your associated physical sensations: Take note of any physical sensations associated with your emotion.

The ADHD brain quickly moves to an upper range of intensity, to emotions closer to the center of Plutchik's Wheel. Was there something you could have done to reduce the intensity of your emotions? If so, what?

What insights have you gained from exploring the intensity of your emotions? How do they affect your mind and body? (For example, I become quickly frustrated by minor annoyances, and it feels like they disrupt my whole body.)

When Emotions Combine

Let's imagine you're feeling annoyance and boredom at work. Your team members talk a lot while you're trying to work, and that annoys you. To make matters worse, your work is monotonous, and you feel bored. Your emotions become more intense and increase to range 7–10. Annoyance expands into anger, and boredom grows into disgust.

Your amygdala is the part of the brain that processes emotions. When you get flooded with feelings of anger and contempt, your amygdala dumps stress hormones into your body as a survival mechanism. Strong emotions—even good ones—can quickly feel overwhelming.

You can start to regulate your less intense emotion of boredom by becoming curious. Look at the complementary emotion of acceptance (across from boredom) on Plutchik's Wheel. Ask yourself, *How can I practice acceptance?*

Though this is difficult to do, thinking through the next step can provide you with deeper understanding of what you might be able to do. Let's say you can come to a place of accepting that, for now, your work is monotonous. Ask yourself, *What is this emotion telling me? Should I prepare to find another job?*

Think about a time when your emotions combined and grew. Tell the story of what happened and how it resolved. In hindsight, what could you have done differently?

_____

_____

_____

_____

_____

_____

_____

_____

_____

_____

Exploring Range of Emotions

Many of us with ADHD feel jolted around by our emotions, zooming between highs and lows. Exploring how you experience different emotional intensities can help you learn to adjust your emotional responses.

Find a calm and quiet place to reflect to complete this activity. Choose an emotion (fear, surprise, sadness, disgust, anger, anticipation, joy, or trust) and complete the chart below.

Emotion: _____

	Feeling this emotion in range 1–3	Feeling this emotion in range 4–6	Feeling this emotion in range 7–10
Thoughts I have when I experience this emotion			
Behaviors I show when I experience this emotion			
Physical sensations I have when I experience this emotion			
What others may experience when I experience this emotion			

Look at your completed graph. Was it difficult for you to complete? If so, why? Most of my clients find that completing the middle portion is the most difficult. Why do you think this is so?

_____

_____

_____

_____

_____

Completing this chart made me . . .

think _____

_____

_____

wish _____

_____

_____

wonder _____

_____

_____

hope _____

_____

_____

decide _____

_____

_____

REINFORCING
YOUR PERSONAL GROWTH

As I did these exercises, I demonstrated curiosity when I

As I did these exercises, I demonstrated courage when I

As I did these exercises, I demonstrated humility when I

As I did these exercises, I demonstrated honesty when I

BIG IDEAS
in Chapter 3

Divergent thinkers have
possibility brains.
Their minds naturally explore
and elaborate on ideas,
examining what *could* be.

4

Following the Rabbit

Many individuals who have ADHD tend to think in a divergent manner, which means that they have a tendency to develop their thoughts in different directions, often simultaneously. This type of thinking is also known as out-of-the-box, nonlinear, or creative thinking, which allows those with ADHD to generate ideas that go beyond conventional thinking or expected limits.

REFLECTION on READING

What do you know now that you didn't before?

_____

_____

_____

What was most interesting to you from this chapter? Why?

_____

_____

_____

What might be a different title for this chapter? Why?

_____

_____

_____

What do you want to know more about now? Why?

_____

_____

_____

What's the most memorable thing from this chapter?

_____

_____

_____

Questions and Exercises

Convergent Thinking

Goal: Find a single best solution to a problem you are trying to solve.
Process: Find the solution by applying established rules and logical reasoning.

Divergent Thinking

Goal: Generate new information, options, or previously undiscovered solutions.
Process: Brainstorm or ask, "What if . . . ?," "Why?," or "How is this idea connected to other ideas?"

The Benefits of a Possibility Brain

Think about how you have used your divergent thinking to look like a rock star. Describe two of those times.

_____

_____

_____

_____

How did it feel when you were using your divergent thinking? What did others say to you?

_____

_____

_____

_____

What aspects of divergent thinking do you use most frequently (creative, original, elaborative, fluent, flexible, or funny)?

_____

_____

_____

In what situations do you find yourself utilizing your possibility brain the most, engaging in divergent thinking? Describe examples from work and home life. How do you feel when you use this type of thinking?

_____

_____

_____

_____

> Although those of us with ADHD are great at divergent thinking, we are tempted to use it at the wrong times.

Where in your life are you frustrated when you either aren't allowed to or can't use your divergent thinking? What happens?

_____

_____

_____

The Problem with Rabbit Holes

If you tend to lean on your divergent thinking patterns, you need to be aware of and understand the cognitive errors you may be prone to make. Explore these common rabbit holes in your divergent thinking.

Using only divergent thinking. Describe a time you relied only on your divergent thinking when convergent thinking was required. What happened? What would you have done differently?

_____

_____

_____

_____

Being interested only in big challenges. It's natural for those of us with ADHD to be attracted to captivating, intricate, and meaningful challenges, but this often comes with a cost. When did you neglect convergent thinking tasks in order to follow the more interesting divergent tasks? What could you do differently?

Being in love with your divergent thinking. I love my divergent thinking. It's fun and entertaining! But if I don't pay attention to the details, projects fail and I let others down. When have you been so in love with your divergent thinking that a project was affected or you left others holding the details? What were the consequences? How did you repair the situation?

Being fixated on your "potential." Have you ever been told how smart you are and how much potential you have? Those comments can create a vacuum in our lives when we never live up to our "potential." In what ways do you believe you haven't lived up to your potential? Counter that thinking by creating a list of things you have accomplished and can be proud of.

Write a note to your ten-year-old self about what you have done and learned now that you are older.

Dealing with imagination plus anxiety. Our wonderfully vivid imaginations combine with our anxiety and fears to create monsters—cognitive distortions that torture us. We let the monsters that we create take over our rational thoughts. Tell about a time when your divergent thinking created even more anxiety.

Having no patience for convergent activities. I hate the household tasks that require slow, uninteresting details. What convergent tasks are you avoiding today? What finally motivates you to do them?

Creating Rube Goldberg machines. Like the American cartoonist Rube Goldberg, I frequently find that I have completed a simple task in an indirect and overly complicated way. So before beginning something, I try to catch myself and ask, "Is this the simplest approach?" Have you caught yourself making a Rube Goldberg machine when a simpler approach would work? Have you seen others do it? How do you stop yourself from making this common cognitive error?

_____

_____

_____

Getting stuck in problem finding. Given our tendency toward imagination and expansive thinking, those of us who depend on divergent thinking are problem-finding geniuses! But problem finding is only the first stage. Eventually we need to shift to convergent problem-solving. Have you found yourself stuck in problem finding? Which step(s) of the problem-solving process below do you tend to get stuck in? Why?

_____

_____

_____

Problem-Solving Process

Step 1: Define the problem.

Step 2: Analyze the problem.

Step 3: Develop potential solutions.

Step 4: Evaluate the options.

Step 5: Select the best option.

Step 6: Implement the solution.

Step 7: Measure the results.

What is your strategy for moving to Steps 6 and 7? If you don't have one, talk with family or friends who are good at deciding on a solution and executing it. Write their strategy here.

_____

_____

_____

_____

Not monitoring your divergent pattern. How many times have I picked up my phone to check an email and gotten lost scrolling and looking at so many other things? It happens when I don't monitor my divergent brain. My mind goes to all the interesting things, and I forget to find the email I was looking for. Oops! This is the most common error of all—we pop down a rabbit hole and forget where we are supposed to be. We need to maintain a meta-awareness of which type of thinking we are using and question if it is effective in the moment.

For those of us with ADHD, this pattern is such a difficult one to break. Start by observing when it occurs. When do you find yourself going down a rabbit hole (e.g., when you search on your computer, pick up your phone, lie down on your big, comfy chair)?

_____

_____

_____

_____

Create awareness around those times. (For example, when I pick up my phone, I say aloud, "I'm looking for the email from Leslie.") What are some strategies you could use when you are standing close to a rabbit hole?

When I _____ and don't want to go down a rabbit hole,

I will _____

When I _____ and don't want to go down a rabbit hole,

I will _____

When I _____ and don't want to go down a rabbit hole,

I will _____

REINFORCING
YOUR PERSONAL GROWTH

While completing this chapter, I maintained a growth mindset by

I am proud of myself because

I surprised myself when

Because my most common divergent error is _____, I will

BIG IDEAS
in Chapter 4

5

The Monsters We Face

Just like Annie in chapter 5 of *Your Brain's Not Broken*, adults with ADHD have monsters too. Two of our natural ADHD tendencies—divergent thinking patterns and lack of emotional regulation—collide to create vicious and scary monsters from everyday occurrences.

Renaissance philosopher Michel de Montaigne seemed to know something about the imagined monsters we face when he wrote, "Who fears to suffer, already suffers what he fears."[1] In other words, when someone worries that something will happen, their mind and body are already experiencing the very thing they are fearing as though it is currently taking place.

REFLECTION on READING

Does Annie remind you of anyone? If so, who and in what way?

_____

_____

_____

What does the story about Annie make you think about?

_____

_____

_____

What is the most memorable thing about this chapter? Why?

_____

_____

_____

Was there something you disagreed with? If so, what? Why?

_____

_____

_____

_____

Questions and Exercises

If you have ADHD, you likely have monsters. Naming the beasts you are facing is the first essential step to managing them or banishing them from your life.

Naming things is built deep into our subconscious. To name a thing is to acknowledge its existence as separate from everything else that has a name. During early childhood development, as a very young child learns to speak, you can see the relief and delight on their face as they name something. Giving something a name makes it real and able to be communicated about in order to transform its strangeness into familiarity.

Name your monsters by addressing your fear. What stresses you out? What makes you feel anxious? What is that thing you worry about?

Sometimes your fear is more generalized or nebulous. Do you have a deep fear of being rejected? Are you afraid of not being worthy of love? Of failing? Of being vulnerable? Of not having the support you need? Of making decisions? Of traveling? Without analyzing it too much, list as many monsters as you can in two minutes. On your mark, set your timer . . . GO!

Look at the list you created. Circle three that are particularly troublesome for you and then add them to the chart below. Although it may feel uncomfortable, complete this table to the best of your ability.

	Monster 1	Monster 2	Monster 3
Describe your monster.			
When does this monster appear?			
Where and how do you feel this in your body?			
How can you calm your body? (See tips below for a few ideas.)			
What thoughts are you having before or during an encounter with this monster?			
What thoughts could you replace them with?			

	Monster 1	Monster 2	Monster 3
Are the new thoughts helpful? More realistic?			
Combine your body-calming technique with your new thoughts, and you've created your monster spray. What is your monster spray (coping skill)? What else do you think you could do to gain more control of the situation?			
Now that you've created your monster spray, how will you remember to use it?			

Some tips for creating your monster spray:

- Remind yourself that the feeling in your body is the fight, flight, or freeze response. It is not dangerous, and you have managed this feeling before.

- Use the *5-4-3-2-1 grounding technique*: Take a deep breath and find
  5 things you can see
  4 things you can touch
  3 things you can hear
  2 things you can smell
  1 thing you can taste

- Try the *box breathing technique*: Slowly, without forcing it, exhale through your mouth for a count of 4; hold for a count of 4; inhale slowly for a count of 4; hold for a count of 4. Repeat for three to five minutes. Some of my clients find it useful to trace a square in the air while breathing to enhance their focus.[2]

REINFORCING
YOUR PERSONAL GROWTH

In this chapter, I thought and wrote about some things that I may not have wanted to. I demonstrated courage when I

As I did these exercises, I demonstrated humility when I

As I did these exercises, I demonstrated honesty when I

I am proud of myself because

Completing these exercises made me decide that

BIG IDEAS
in Chapter 5

The key to getting things done
is to see the emotions involved
and learn to redirect them.

6

Malicious Motivation

Many of us with ADHD struggle to initiate tasks, especially those deemed tedious or routine, and we often need to engage our emotional brains to begin. Unlike those without ADHD, we are less likely to have dependable access to the prefrontal cortex, which manages life's details calmly and rationally, like a butler managing the details of a house. Consequently, we often rely on our emotional centers in the limbic system to remember, make decisions, and motivate ourselves, utilizing emotions as aids in thinking, planning, and acting. Let's examine which of the malicious motivators you use to complete tasks.

REFLECTION on READING

After reading this chapter,

I felt _____ because _____

_____

_____

_____

I wondered why _____

_____

_____

_____

I realized that _____

_____

_____

_____

I decided that _____

_____

_____

_____

Confronting Harmful Motivation

As you wake up each day, imagine that your life battery is fully charged. You are hopeful and are ready to take on the day. But as the day goes by, your charge slowly declines. Each poor emotional motivational technique you use (avoidance, anxiety, procrastination, anger, shame, and self-loathing) drains your battery rapidly and leaves you feeling physically and emotionally exhausted. Malicious motivation is costly to you.

Address the emotional manipulations you use to motivate yourself. Breaking the pattern of using them takes commitment to retraining your brain. It is going to take work to learn new habits of thinking, but you will be able to do it.

If you already understand what motivational strategies you are employing, complete the charts below. If you are not certain which ones you use, try this experiment: Set an alarm for an hour from now. When it goes off, write down an emotional trick you used or were tempted to use during that time, whether at work or at home. Set the alarm again and repeat. Look for patterns in your thinking.

Enlist the support of a trusted confidant. Ask your spouse or a close friend to give you feedback about your use of these tactics. Listen carefully and write down their observations of your motivation.

Emotional tricks you used:

_____

_____

_____

Rate the frequency of your current usage for these malicious motivators.

Malicious Motivator	Hourly (5 points)	Daily (4 points)	Weekly (3 points)	Monthly (2 points)	Infrequently (1 point)	Almost Never (0 points)
Avoidance						
Anxiety						
Procrastination						
Anger						
Shame						
Self-Loathing						

Now rate the duration of your use of them. How long do you tend to remain stuck in each one?

When I use this malicious motivator . . .	I really don't get a break from using it (5 points)	I feel stuck for at least a day, and then I can get to the task, but I will still use the motivator during the task (4 points)	I feel stuck for at least three hours, and then I can get to the task, but I'm tempted to use the motivator while I work (3 points)	I feel stuck for at least an hour, and then I can get to the task (2 points)	I feel stuck for at least half an hour, and then I can get to the task (1 point)	I feel stuck for a few minutes, and then I can get to the task (0 points)
Avoidance						
Anxiety						
Procrastination						
Anger						
Shame						
Self-Loathing						

Score the two tables by combining the number next to the category you chose. For example, if you chose "Weekly (3 points)" from the frequency chart and "I feel stuck for at least an hour, and then I can get to the task (2 points)" from the duration chart, your score would be 5.

Malicious Motivator	Score
Avoidance	
Anxiety	
Procrastination	
Anger	
Shame	
Self-Loathing	

You can use these scores as a guide to help you choose which malicious motivator to address first. If you have a score of 8 or more in a category, you may want to talk to an ADHD professional. A coach or counselor who is specifically trained in the area of ADHD can help you acknowledge, address, and stop using these strategies.

Common ADHD Motivational Traps

Many adults with ADHD feel the need to hijack the emotional part of their brain to get started on a task, especially one they find tedious, uninteresting, or routine.

Avoidance: You'd Rather Be Doing Something Else

Avoidance is very common in all people, not just those of us with ADHD. We use the avoidance tactic to motivate ourselves to do things other than the important task before us. Avoidance often lets us feel productive by accomplishing something, even though it is not what needs to be done.

Take a moment to think about what you are avoiding (a task, a conversation, etc.). If you aren't currently avoiding anything, try to remember a specific time when you were. Consider the following questions:

What are you (or what were you) truly avoiding?

_____

_____

Why are you (or why were you) avoiding this thing?

_____

_____

Check in with your emotions. Are you avoiding this thing because it makes you feel uncomfortable? Or because it makes you feel another emotion? Try to name the emotion. Look at Plutchik's Wheel of Emotion, figure 3.1 at the back of the book, to help you locate the emotion.

_____

_____

_____

_____

What can you do with that emotion instead of avoiding it? (If the emotions are too intense, please see a mental health professional who understands ADHD.)

_____

_____

_____

Check in with your body. What are your physical sensations when you think about this task (stomachache, shoulder pain, etc.)? Are you fleeing because your nervous system is activated and stressed? Why do you think your body considers this task dangerous to you?

_____

_____

_____

How can you soothe, care for, or move your body to remind it you are safe and okay even if you are uncomfortable or stressed? There are many strategies you can use to calm your nervous system. A quick internet search will yield many options. Find the one that is right for you.

_____

_____

_____

How is avoidance trying to serve you? Are you using it to get other undesirable tasks done? Are you justifying your avoidance?

_____

_____

_____

Reality check. What is the real priority of this thing you are avoiding? What is the cost or consequence of not addressing it? Do you believe or hope that if you don't do this task, it will just resolve on its own? Will it resolve without you addressing it?

_____

_____

_____

_____

Many times, we use common ADHD motivational traps because it is difficult for us to delineate the steps we need to take in order to accomplish a task. Complete this prompt:

If I were to do this task, here are the first five steps I would need to take:

1. _____

_____

2. _____

_____

3. _____

_____

4. _____

_____

5. _____

_____

Anxiety: The Tyranny of the Urgent

We use anxiety to increase performance. It makes us move and take action. When we forget things that aren't in our focus, anxious thoughts hold them in our memory. The anxiety-alerting system works something like this: A woman gets out of her car and says to herself, "I need to remember to lock my car." Her thoughts race on. *I need to listen for the beep. What if I double-clicked my key fob and it actually unlocked the car? Someone could steal my stuff. What is in my car? Oh, my son's iPad. I don't want that stolen. He would be furious—and I can't buy a new one right now. Lock car.* Anxiety makes her lock her car.

Individuals with ADHD compensate for a lack of focus with racing thoughts, nervousness, and worry. This is especially true for those with undiagnosed or untreated ADHD. If our logical motivation is a faint flame reminding us that we should get to a task, we pour gasoline—anxiety—on that flame and we are motivated. The drawback, as it is with each of our emotional tricks, is that motivating ourselves with anxiety is exhausting.

> **Reminder:** Using anxiety to motivate yourself and having an anxiety disorder are not the same. Please see an ADHD-informed therapist if you have been diagnosed with generalized anxiety disorder or another type of anxiety disorder.

Take a moment to think about what you are anxious about (a task, a conversation, etc.). If you aren't currently anxious about anything, try to remember a specific time when you were. Consider the following questions:

What are you (or what were you) truly feeling anxious about?

_____

_____

Why are you (or why were you) anxious about this thing? Are you worried about forgetting to do it? Does it seem extremely important to complete as soon as possible? Why does it feel this way?

_____

_____

Check in with your emotions. Are you anxious about this thing because it makes you feel uncomfortable? Or because it makes you feel another emotion? Try to name the emotion. Look at Plutchik's Wheel of Emotion, figure 3.1 at the back of the book, to help you locate the emotion.

What can you do with that emotion instead of feeling anxious about it? (If the emotions are too intense, please see a mental health professional who understands ADHD.)

Check in with your body. What are your physical sensations when you think about this task (stomachache, shoulder pain, etc.)? Are you anxious because your nervous system is activated and stressed? Why do you think your body considers this task dangerous to you?

How can you soothe, care for, or move your body to remind it you are safe and okay even if you are uncomfortable or stressed? There are many strategies that you can use to calm your nervous system. A quick internet search will yield many options. Find the one that is right for you.

How is this feeling of anxiousness trying to serve you? Are you using it to get other undesirable tasks done? Are you justifying your anxiety?

_____

_____

_____

_____

Reality check. What is the real priority of this task? What will happen if it doesn't go "perfectly" or the way you want it to?

_____

_____

_____

_____

Many times, we use common ADHD motivational traps because it is difficult for us to delineate the steps we need to take in order to accomplish a task. Complete this prompt:

If I were to do this task, here are the first five steps I would need to take:

1. _____

_____

2. _____

_____

3. _____

_____

4. _____

_____

5. _____

_____

Procrastination: It's Like You're Dodging a Bullet

Procrastination, like avoidance, is a way of diverting interest to initiate a task, but with anxiety added. Here is how it works: I need to do a particular task, but there is no reason to do it immediately, so I wait. And wait. And wait—until it becomes impossible to accomplish on time. Then, like a superhero—ka-POW!—anxiety rushes in and the task finally gets done.

Delaying tasks to feel motivated doesn't lead to our best work. However, it does create pressure to get things done. If procrastination often works for you, you might start thinking it's necessary to accomplish anything. After procrastinating, some people celebrate their achievement while others feel ashamed. Many get used to the feeling of narrowly avoiding a problem, and it can become a sort of thrill.

How do you feel after finishing a task you put off? Has this strategy ever failed you?

We all procrastinate at times, and the reasons we do so are endless. What happens when you keep procrastinating on important stuff? How have you suffered consequences from procrastination?

Check in with your emotions. What happens to your emotional energy level when you procrastinate? Do you feel depleted or energized after completing a task that you procrastinated?

Describe your thoughts after completing a task that you procrastinated.

_____

_____

_____

_____

Check in with your body. What happens in your body when you procrastinate (increased heart rate, muscle tension, etc.)?

_____

_____

Reality check. Do you really want to stop using this malicious motivational technique? Why or why not?

_____

_____

Are you currently putting off a task that you should be doing? Are you procrastinating out of fear or overwhelm? What are you afraid of? Why does it seem overwhelming? (Remember to embrace your growth mindset from page 10.)

_____

_____

_____

_____

Many times, we use common ADHD motivational traps because we feel overwhelmed, and it is difficult for us to delineate the steps we need to take in order to accomplish a task. We can sometimes move ourselves out of procrastination when we figure out three things: (1) exactly what we need to do, (2) how to do it, and (3) when to do it.

If I were to do this task, here are the first five steps I would need to take:

1. _____

_____

2. _____

_____

3. _____

_____

4. _____

_____

5. _____

_____

If you can't write out the steps, then figure out what you need to know to get moving. Find a resource—an expert in the field, a friend, a webinar, an online course, a book, a website—to give you the skills you need to get the task done.

Look at the first step you wrote. Can you do it? Is it still too big? Try breaking it down into even smaller steps.

1. _____

_____

2. _____

_____

3. _____

_____

4. _____

_____

5. _____

_____

Now try accomplishing the first few small steps. How does it feel? Motivation often follows action, not the other way around. Start the task, and you may find that you become more motivated as you make progress.

_____

_____

_____

_____

Find a place on your calendar to schedule time to complete a few of the next steps. How does it feel?

_____

_____

_____

_____

▨ PROCRASTINATING BECAUSE OF PERFECTIONISM

Procrastinating because of perfectionism happens when people put off tasks because they fear not doing them perfectly. I still struggle with perfectionism in certain areas of my life. I set very high standards for myself and get worried about making mistakes or not reaching those standards. This fear can stop me from starting or finishing tasks.

How about you? In what ways have you been a procrastinating perfectionist?

_____

_____

_____

_____

While wanting things to be perfect can help produce great work, it can also make it hard to finish things on time. To overcome this type of procrastination, it's important for us to set more realistic goals, understand that perfection is impossible, and learn to appreciate the effort put into tasks rather than just focusing on making everything perfect. Changing the way we see mistakes and imperfections is critical to breaking the cycle of procrastination linked to the pursuit of perfection.

What problems does perfectionism cause for you?

_____

_____

_____

_____

Is perfectionism helpful in any way? If so, how?

_____

_____

_____

_____

How do you feel about giving up the unhelpful aspects of perfectionism?

_____

_____

_____

_____

How will your life be better if you can be less perfectionistic?

_____

_____

_____

_____

▦ PERFECTIONISM IS A BULLY IN YOUR BRAIN

Those of us who strive for perfection are often unkind to ourselves. We set too-high standards and then criticize ourselves when we can't reach them. We say things to ourselves that we wouldn't speak to someone else. The questions below can help you shift your negative self-talk.

Check in with your thoughts. What kinds of negative things does your inner perfectionist say to you?

_____

_____

_____

In what ways do you consider your negative self-talk helpful? How do you use your negative self-talk to hold yourself to a higher standard?

_____

_____

_____

How can you respond to your inner perfectionist's expectations, demands, and criticisms with understanding and compassion?

_____

_____

_____

What do you think your inner perfectionist is afraid of?

_____

_____

_____

Reality check. What do you think your perfectionism is trying to protect you from?

_____

_____

_____

What are you afraid will happen if you stop trying to be perfect?

If you did stop trying to be perfect, how might your life be better?

What can you say to remind yourself that you are enough just as you are?

As procrastinating perfectionists, we often spend too much time trying to make things perfect, even when it's unnecessary. We need to constantly work, and we're so focused on doing more, doing it perfectly, and attempting to be everything for everyone that we forget to relax and enjoy ourselves. Tell about the last time you spent tinkering with something well past completion. What do you wish you would have done differently? What can you do differently now?

What are you giving up because your perfectionism tells you to work harder, do more, and prove yourself?

_____

_____

_____

_____

As perfectionists, we tend to focus on the negatives. We notice only our deficits and failures, never our strengths and successes. We worry about everything that could go wrong. We think in black-and-white, failing to see that good enough really is good enough.

What are your strengths?

_____

_____

_____

_____

When have you done something well but not perfectly?

_____

_____

_____

_____

How can you enjoy the process or experience of something rather than focusing only on the outcome?

_____

_____

_____

_____

Anger: Getting Mad Moves You to Action

Feeling angry can sometimes give us the push we need to tackle a lingering task we've been avoiding for a while. The surge of anger can make us feel empowered and driven to accomplish what we've been putting off.

However, while anger is a natural emotion that helps us process our feelings, release tension, and manage difficult emotions, using it as motivation can have downsides. It may steer us away from our goals and have negative consequences. When anger makes us feel like we're not in control, we are more likely to make impulsive decisions and give in to harmful impulses. It can even contribute to giving up on our goals. Additionally, anger may worsen feelings of depression, creating a sense of helplessness and hopelessness and diminishing our confidence.

Check in with your emotions. What is the source of your anger?

What is causing you to be upset?

What can you do to deal with the source of your anger?

Reality check. Describe how your anger-driven motivation is affecting your self-perception. Is it making you feel better or worse about yourself?

Sometimes we use anger to do something that will help us meet our goals. Think of a time when you were motivated to do something out of spite, irritation, or anger.

Describe the effect your irritation or anger had on others.

_____

_____

_____

In what ways does your anger get in the way of being the person you want to be?

_____

_____

_____

Is your motivational anger directed at yourself or other people? Or is it just providing a burst of focus and energy to help get the job done? What is the effect of this on you and others?

_____

_____

_____

Review your answers to the previous questions. Set rules to protect yourself and others when you use anger to motivate. (For example: "I am not allowed to have an emotional outburst when I am trying to motivate myself.")

_____

_____

_____

Shame and Self-Loathing: Motivation through Disgust at Yourself

The last dirty emotional tricks that those of us with ADHD use to accomplish tasks are even more dastardly and exhausting than the previous ones. We turn to shame and self-loathing as strategies when the others fail. These tools require us to increase the frequency and duration of our intense emotions. Shame and self-loathing aren't turned on briefly like the previous tricks of avoidance, anxiety, procrastination, and anger. Instead, these dirty emotional tricks often act like chronic inflammation, a constant irritation to our emotional sense of well-being.

Shame and self-loathing often rely on a hostile internal dialogue. If you use this trick to motivate yourself, it can be very difficult to see your pattern. To help you identify how you may be trying to use this malicious motivator, check each box that applies to you:

- ☐ Do you often criticize yourself?
- ☐ Do you struggle to accept compliments?
- ☐ Do you frequently use negative labels to describe yourself?
- ☐ Do you blame yourself for everything?
- ☐ Do you judge yourself harshly?
- ☐ Do you believe your negative thoughts?
- ☐ Do you compare yourself to others often?
- ☐ Do you have trouble forgiving yourself?
- ☐ Do you fear failure and avoid taking risks?
- ☐ Do you believe you are not good enough?

Reflect on the boxes that you checked. How are these beliefs and behaviors holding you back from accomplishing what you want?

_____

_____

_____

How are these beliefs and behaviors holding you back from loving people better?

_____

_____

_____

How are these beliefs and behaviors holding you back from self-acceptance?

_____

_____

_____

_____

Can you recall a recent negative inner dialogue? What were you saying to yourself?

_____

_____

_____

_____

Do you judge others this harshly, or just yourself? What do you want to do about that?

_____

_____

_____

_____

If you can, give a brief description of a recent situation in which you used shame and self-loathing to motivate yourself. Where were you? What time of day was it? What happened prior to the situation? What was happening when you became aware of your negative self-talk?

_____

_____

_____

_____

Check in with your thoughts. Using the questions above to guide you, identify one core negative belief you have about yourself. Although there may be many, focus on one limiting belief at a time. (For example: "I'm not good enough, and that's why I'm not able to finish college.")

How do you think this thought came to be lodged in your mind? Does something remind you of it in your daily life?

Describe when and how this belief isn't accurate. Look for specific examples in your past where you have proven this belief wrong. It can be something big or small.

Showing compassion to others is often easier than showing it to ourselves. Thinking about what you may say to others in a similar situation can help you realize how hard you might be on yourself. Start by imagining the advice you would give to someone else in your situation. What is good about that advice? What elements of it can you apply to yourself?

Write down specific steps you can take to apply the advice for a friend to yourself.

_____

_____

_____

_____

Write a note to yourself about what you want to change in your thinking. What positive affirmations can you say to yourself when this negative thought comes up?

If these exercises were difficult for you and you need additional support, please seek the guidance of an ADHD-informed therapist. Therapy can be incredibly valuable and can help you on your personal growth journey.

REINFORCING
YOUR PERSONAL GROWTH

Why is it important for me to address these common ADHD motivational traps? What is the cost of using them?

What are some simple steps I could take to avoid my most common malicious motivator?

Who or what could support me as I make this change?

How can I positively motivate myself instead?

It is reasonable to ask, "If I can't use these malicious strategies, then what can I do to motivate myself?" Each of us needs to find our own successful strategies. What works for me may not work for you. You will need to create your individual "owner's manual" to spark interest that leads to action. Capture ideas that can help you use different strategies.

BIG IDEAS
in Chapter 6

7

Solving Motivational Murders

Motivation can be challenging for individuals with ADHD due to their perception of time and their tendency to prioritize enjoyable tasks over important ones. To boost motivation, it's crucial to understand our brain's workings, recognize our strengths, and develop strategies to set realistic goals, prioritize tasks, and create a supportive environment.

REFLECTION on READING

What is one insight that you had about yourself or ADHD as you read this chapter? Why was it significant for you?

_____

_____

_____

_____

_____

What are some questions you have after reading this chapter?

_____

_____

_____

_____

_____

A Big Ball of Wibbly-Wobbly, Timey-Wimey

ADHD time blindness can be quite disruptive to normal life functioning. What does it feel like for you?

_____

_____

_____

Which statement most closely aligns with your feelings on time?

Time is:

1. My friend. We work well together. I understand it and use it well.
2. A frenemy. Although I know it is not my enemy, I have a fundamental dislike of it.
3. An archenemy. I try to manage it effectively, but doing so often feels like a battle, and time will inevitably work against me.
4. A trickster. I feel like it is an illusion and it deliberately sets out to deceive me.
5. A pretenemy. I have a complex relationship with it. I pretend to hate it and not have enough of it, but I actually don't hate it.
6. _____

Describe your relationship with time. Why did you choose the answer above?

_____

_____

_____

What tasks do you think will take less time than they actually do?

_____

_____

_____

What tasks do you think will take more time than they actually do?

_____

_____

_____

_____

What strategies do you currently use to manage your time blindness? Do they work?

_____

_____

_____

_____

Curious and Shiny

Fun things get our attention, and therefore fun tasks get done. We are captivated by excitement and amusement, so our brains search the horizon for the interesting, the shiny, the curious, the remarkable, the exciting—and call it all "fun." This principle affects our level of drive, our motivation, our happiness, and even our sense of well-being.

Have you ever thought of yourself as a fun seeker? Describe how you seek fun.

_____

_____

_____

_____

Sometimes being a fun seeker pays off. In what ways does it help you?

_____

_____

_____

_____

Sometimes being a fun seeker gets us in trouble. In what ways does it not help you?

_____

_____

_____

The Energy Drain

Use these charts to track your energy levels over three days. Pick at least one day where your schedule is more your own, with no classes or work. Some of my clients set alarms to help them complete this exercise.

Day: _____ **Date:** _____

		6–8 a.m.	8–10 a.m.	10 a.m.–12 p.m.	12–2 p.m.	2–4 p.m.	4–6 p.m.	6–8 p.m.	8–10 p.m.	10 p.m.–12 a.m.
Maximum energy	10									
	9									
	8									
	7									
	6									
	5									
	4									
	3									
	2									
	1									
Minimum energy	0									

Day: _____ **Date:** _____

		6–8 a.m.	8–10 a.m.	10 a.m.–12 p.m.	12–2 p.m.	2–4 p.m.	4–6 p.m.	6–8 p.m.	8–10 p.m.	10 p.m.–12 a.m.
Maximum energy	**10**									
	9									
	8									
	7									
	6									
	5									
	4									
	3									
	2									
	1									
Minimum energy	0									

Day: _____ **Date:** _____

		6–8 a.m.	8–10 a.m.	10 a.m.–12 p.m.	12–2 p.m.	2–4 p.m.	4–6 p.m.	6–8 p.m.	8–10 p.m.	10 p.m.–12 a.m.
Maximum energy	**10**									
	9									
	8									
	7									
	6									
	5									
	4									
	3									
	2									
	1									
Minimum energy	0									

Now look over your charts. What time of day do you tend to have more energy? Can you use that time to get the "difficult" things done?

_____

_____

_____

_____

Do you notice any differences between the workday and the nonwork day?

_____

_____

_____

_____

What types of activities drain your energy?

_____

_____

_____

_____

What types of activities give you energy?

_____

_____

_____

_____

Perceived Energy and Actual Energy*

Our motivation is also affected by the amount of physical energy we *perceive* a task will require. We come to this conclusion by assigning each task a feeling, then through the lens of our hyperarousal, we gauge the difficulty of that task and how much energy it will use. As with our estimations of time, we tend to overestimate or underestimate the amount of energy we will need.

Create an awareness of your perceived energy versus actual energy. Try this activity:

1. Think about a task that you know you need to do but don't really want to do (e.g., answering an email, weeding the garden). What is your perceived energy to do this task? (1 = no energy/motivation, 10 = high energy/motivation) _____

2. Set your timer for ten minutes and begin the task. (I know you don't want to do it, but this is for science.)

3. When the timer goes off, mark your current energy. (1 = no energy/motivation, 10 = high energy/motivation) _____

4. Did your energy increase or decrease? If it increased, can you finish the task? If it decreased, what do you need to do to take care of your body (e.g., sleep, drink water)? Write your observations here:

_____

_____

_____

_____

Repeat this exercise so you can become aware of your *perceived* energy and your *actual* energy.

*For your convenience, the worksheet on this page is also available on pages 170–71 for easy reference and copying.

REINFORCING
YOUR PERSONAL GROWTH

As I did these exercises, I demonstrated humility when I

As I did these exercises, I demonstrated honesty when I

As I did these exercises, I retained a growth mindset by

BIG IDEAS
in Chapter 7

8

Living on the Grid

The Solve-It Grid helps you engage with tasks, tolerate emotional discomfort, and switch modes of working. It's a powerful tool that can assist you in overcoming procrastination, managing difficult emotions, and adapting to changing circumstances. Read through figure 8.1 at the back of the book. Is there a part of the drawing that made you laugh because you recognized yourself? Or made you cringe because you've felt that?

REFLECTION on READING

What connections did you make while reading this chapter?

_____

_____

_____

What information was already familiar to you?

_____

_____

_____

What two important things will you remember from this chapter?

_____

_____

_____

Questions and Exercises

The Solve-It Grid

The Solve-It Grid is based on two ADHD inclinations:

- *Perception of interest.* This is the degree to which a person with ADHD considers how fun an activity will be when deciding how to accomplish a task.
- *Emotional intensity.* This is the degree to which a person with ADHD calculates how much emotional energy a task will take.

The Solve-It Grid

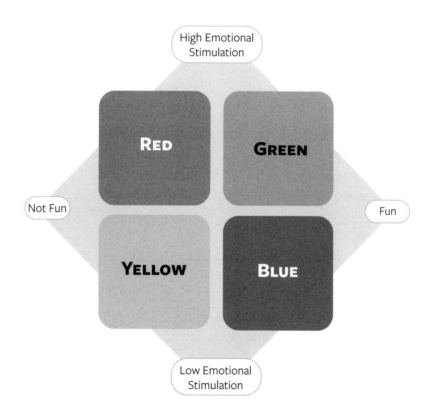

You can see a color version of the Solve-It Grid, figure 8.2, at the back of the book.

Practice Awareness

One of the most important things you can do to manage your ADHD is to manage your energy expenditures. A way to increase your awareness of those levels is by assessing how different activities affect your energy. As you find yourself in a task or activity, ask:

1. Is this task or activity fun or not fun?
2. How emotionally stimulating is this task or activity?
3. How is my energy increasing or decreasing with this task or activity?
4. In which color quadrant is this task or activity located?

Learn about Your Grid

Having trouble? Move the task or activity around the grid until you find its accurate placement.

Tasks that are usually in the Yellow Quadrant for you are

_____

_____

_____

_____

What is it about these tasks that makes them Yellow for you?

_____

_____

_____

_____

Tasks that are usually in the Red Quadrant for you are

_____

_____

_____

_____

What is it about these tasks that makes them Red for you?

_____

_____

_____

_____

Tasks that are usually in the Blue Quadrant for you are

_____

_____

_____

_____

What is it about these tasks that makes them Blue for you?

_____

_____

_____

_____

Tasks that are usually in the Green Quadrant for you are

_____

_____

_____

_____

What is it about these tasks that makes them Green for you?

_____

_____

_____

_____

Focus on the Yellow Quadrant*

Many of us with ADHD have difficulty with the Yellow Quadrant. Try this exercise and increase your resilience in this quadrant.

Select a Yellow task that you need to accomplish today. Use the following questions to help you tackle this and other Yellow tasks.

Task: _____

What makes this a Yellow task for you?

_____

_____

_____

_____

Why does it need to be done?

_____

_____

_____

_____

When do you want to begin the task? (Block out the time on your calendar.)

_____

_____

_____

_____

*For your convenience, the worksheets on pages 100–102 are also available on pages 172–77 for easy reference and copying.

Plan how you will accomplish this task. Be specific. Write a how-to list of the steps you need to take.

Look at your how-to list and plan how you will actually begin. Where will you work? What will you need around you?

How will you handle distractions and get back on track? What might be emotionally distracting to you while you work? How will you manage that? How will you guard yourself against malicious motivators?

How will you know when you are finished? (This step helps you avoid the perfection trap.)

Set a timer for twenty minutes or less. Then begin the task.

1. When the timer alerts you, take a deep breath. How are you doing? What do you notice? (If you have hit a great rhythm with your task, congratulations! Keep going! If not, go to the next step.)

2. What is blocking you from completing this task? Check the box below.

   ☐ An emotional reason (e.g., you just hate this work so much that you don't want to do it)

   ☐ A technical reason (e.g., you don't have the information you need)

   ☐ A cognitive reason (e.g., you don't understand how to complete the task)

Explain why you checked the box you did.

_____

_____

_____

If you have an *emotional reason*, try taking a short break and go to a timed Blue Quadrant activity. Attempt the task again after the break.

If you have a *technical reason*, write down what you need in order to complete the task. Rewrite your how-to list. Set the timer again.

If you have a *cognitive reason*, write down what you don't understand or know. How will you learn what you need to know? What resources could you use to fill in this gap? Rewrite your how-to list. Set the timer again.

Which strategy are you going to try?

_____

_____

_____

_____

When You Finish the Yellow Task

Congratulate yourself. You did it! You conquered a task that you were tempted to avoid or procrastinate. Write yourself a congratulatory note that honestly commends you for pushing through and finishing this task. (If you are like me, you will be tempted to add sarcasm to this note. Please don't. We're trying to get rid of the negative talk—even when it's humorous.)

What went well for you? What did you do that helped you complete this task?

How can you remember to use this strategy with your next Yellow task?

REINFORCING
YOUR PERSONAL GROWTH

While completing this chapter, I maintained a growth mindset by

I am proud of myself because

I surprised myself when

When I have a Yellow task, I will try this strategy:

BIG IDEAS
in Chapter 8

One of the ways that we can
manage our ADHD is
to watch for what patterns
we are using and to address
them the best we can.

9

Predictable Patterns

For those of us with ADHD, mindfully managing our battery usage helps us accomplish more tasks and feel better about ourselves. Unfortunately, we get stuck in behavior patterns that keep us from using our resources well. Our unconscious patterns feel comfortable to us, so we don't realize how damaging they are to our energy levels, productivity, and relationships. We can use the Solve-It Grid to help evaluate our mistaken beliefs, create better habits, and improve our performance. When we examine our behavior in the different quadrants, we learn what ensnares our thinking.

REFLECTION on READING

What confused you about what you read? As you read further, did your confusion dissipate? Why or why not?

_____

_____

_____

_____

As you read this chapter, were there times when you thought, "Ouch, I do that!" or "Ugh, that sounds familiar"? Find the specific phrase or example that caused that type of reaction and write it below.

_____

_____

_____

_____

What is something from this chapter you would like to share with someone else? Why?

_____

_____

_____

_____

Questions and Exercises

To help you discover your own predictable patterns, take the four quizzes below.

The Need for Speed Quiz

See how you score on the Need for Speed pattern. Check each box that applies to you:

☐ Do you always seem to have a crisis going in your life (real or overblown)?

☐ Does getting angry help you work better?

☐ Are you always rushing, with a packed schedule?

☐ Would others say that you often have dramatic conflicts or outbursts of intense emotion?

☐ Do you feel guilty if you use your spare time to relax?

☐ Do you need to win to derive enjoyment from games and sports?

☐ Do you generally move, walk, and eat rapidly?

☐ Are your physical movements hurried?

☐ Do you thrive or feel exhilarated under pressure?

☐ Do you (or others) consider yourself a high achiever?

The Playing with Fire Quiz

See how you score on the Playing with Fire pattern. Check each box that applies to you:

☐ Do you often find yourself rushing to complete important tasks that you had intended to do days before?

☐ Do you delay simple tasks that require little more than sitting down and doing them?

☐ Do you often waste time doing other things when you are trying to prepare for a deadline?

☐ Are you constantly saying, "I'll do it tomorrow"?

☐ Do you waste a lot of time on trivial matters before getting to a decision?

☐ Even after you make a decision, do you usually delay acting on it?

☐ Do you find yourself constantly running out of time?

☐ Is your fear of making mistakes stopping you from getting started?

☐ Do you often make excuses for not doing your best work?

☐ Do you wish you could take a break and have some relaxing fun without guilt?

The Red, Blue, and Back Again Quiz

See how you score on the Red, Blue, and Back Again pattern. Check each box that applies to you:

- ☐ Are you very competitive and self-critical, only to suddenly flip and become complacent?
- ☐ Do you strive relentlessly toward goals without feeling a sense of joy in your efforts or accomplishments?
- ☐ Do you find at times that you know you should be doing something productive but are too fatigued mentally or physically to do anything at all, only to press yourself into hyper-action a day or two later?
- ☐ Do you get wound up quickly and overreact sometimes, but other times you just don't care?
- ☐ Do you experience a driving, persistent sense of urgency to complete tasks?
- ☐ Do you find yourself flipping between being incredibly impatient on some days and very tolerant on others?
- ☐ Do you look like you have two speeds: on and off?
- ☐ Do you sometimes forget to enjoy the journey?
- ☐ When you realize that you forgot to enjoy the journey, does that make you feel sad or down?
- ☐ Although you know you should take more time to relax, do you find that idea unappealing?
- ☐ Do you stop and rest only when your body tells you that you must (through sickness, fatigue, etc.)?

The Nothin' but Blue Quiz

See how you score on the Nothin' but Blue pattern. Check each box that applies to you:

- ☐ Do you question why tasks have to be so difficult all the time?
- ☐ Do you find yourself waiting for inspiration before starting important tasks, and while you wait you might as well _____ [insert Blue activity]?
- ☐ Do you know what you have to do but frequently find yourself spending time doing something else that is more enjoyable?
- ☐ When tired, do you really just want to veg out rather than tackle any of the difficult tasks you face?
- ☐ Do you see how workaholics don't enjoy life, so you refuse to be one?
- ☐ Do you think that if you forgo the small things that make you happy, then you will become a boring, lifeless drone?
- ☐ Do you think that even if you tried to _____ [insert task], you wouldn't know where to start?
- ☐ Do you often imagine people criticizing your work before you even complete it?
- ☐ Can social situations be very uncomfortable for you, and you fear being rejected or criticized?
- ☐ Are you reluctant to take risks or engage in new activities that may prove embarrassing?

Finding Your Pattern

Now, add up the check marks for all four quizzes.

Pattern	Need for Speed	Playing with Fire	Red, Blue, and Back Again	Nothin' but Blue
Total				

Which pattern do you use the most? If there is a tie, think about when each pattern occurs.

_____

_____

_____

_____

Can you remember when you first started using this pattern? How did it seem to help you then?

_____

_____

_____

_____

Why is this pattern problematic for you now? What happens to your battery?

_____

_____

_____

_____

How is this pattern related to the top malicious motivators you identified on page 61?

_____

_____

_____

_____

Identifying Your False Beliefs

One of the ways that we can manage our ADHD is to watch for what patterns we are using and address them the best we can. This is difficult work because it takes a concerted effort to expose our false beliefs and practice better habits. And each pattern is based on false beliefs.

For many of my clients, identifying their limiting thoughts and beliefs is the most challenging part of addressing their Solve-It Grid pattern. ADHD-informed therapists and coaches can offer great support if you can't identify yours.

From reading this chapter, with which false beliefs did you resonate? How do these affect you on a daily basis?

_____

_____

_____

_____

Locating False Beliefs

A quick way that I've found to locate my false beliefs is to think about people I know and what character traits of theirs irritate me. Try this exercise to see if a false belief surfaces for you.

Think about your partner, family members, close friends, or coworkers and identify things that you can't stand or that make you upset every time you see them.

_____

_____

_____

_____

_____

_____

Think of what you wrote like a mirror that reflects your own limiting thoughts. Turn those criticisms around as if you are saying them about yourself. For example, if you wrote, "I hate how Bob always tries to make a task fun," why does that bother you? Is it because you do the same thing? Perhaps you know that you frequently get distracted with Green tasks and neglect Yellow ones.

Or do you believe the opposite of what you see Bob doing? If so, you might say, "I don't allow myself to make things fun. I turn up my anxiety (or anger) to get things done. And he should too."

Did any limiting thoughts and beliefs surface? If so, how might they be related to your Solve-It Grid pattern? If they're not related to the grid, are they related to your malicious motivators from chapter 6? How are these beliefs affecting your motivation or ability to complete tasks?

Addressing Your Pattern

What morning practices do you want to do? At what time will you normally do them? How will you remember to do them?

What midday practices do you want to do? At what time will you normally do them? How will you remember to do them?

_____

_____

_____

_____

What evening practices do you want to do? At what time will you normally do them? How will you remember to do them?

_____

_____

_____

_____

REINFORCING
YOUR PERSONAL GROWTH

As I did these exercises, I demonstrated curiosity when I

As I did these exercises, I demonstrated courage when I

As I did these exercises, I demonstrated humility when I

As I did these exercises, I demonstrated honesty when I

BIG IDEAS
in Chapter 9

10

Climbing the Ladder

Cultivating Emotional Health

The ADHD Emotional Health Ladder helps us see the dynamic interaction between our ADHD, emotions, and behavior. It is composed of five levels: two healthier levels, one average level, and two unhealthy levels. The healthiest traits appear at the top of the ladder. As we descend, we pass progressively through each rung of emotional health. Accurately assessing which rung of the Emotional Health Ladder we are on helps us observe ourselves and address our behavior.

REFLECTION on READING

What was difficult for you to understand in this chapter? Why?

_____

_____

_____

_____

What was new information for you?

_____

_____

_____

_____

What emotions came up while you read this chapter?

_____

_____

_____

_____

Where are you currently on the ADHD Emotional Health Ladder?

_____

_____

_____

_____

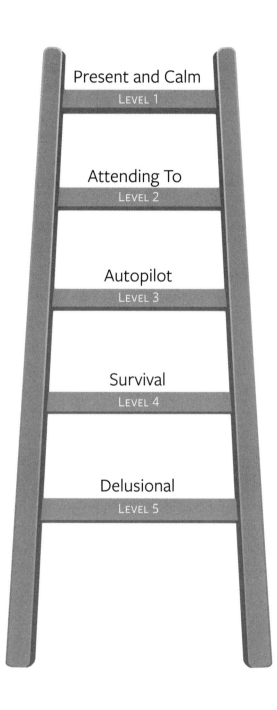

Present and Calm
LEVEL 1

Attending To
LEVEL 2

Autopilot
LEVEL 3

Survival
LEVEL 4

Delusional
LEVEL 5

Level 3: Autopilot

Level 3 is called Autopilot because we aren't consciously controlling our thoughts, attitudes, and behaviors. We move through the day by responding to all the urgent needs that appear before us. Although we may not be as strategic in handling them as we could be, we feel productive because we get tasks accomplished.

Think of a specific time when you were at Level 3 on the Emotional Health Ladder, and consider the questions below. If you can't recall enough information to answer, either ask a close friend or a family member or wait until you experience this level and then complete the questions.

Awareness and attention. We are driven by compulsive, unconscious drives, and our ability to use our radar to assess ourselves and our surroundings is low. We make decisions impulsively. The goal is to solve an immediate problem while not necessarily using strategy. Our focus is on action and productivity. We often say and do things to try to gain control over situations that feel chaotic.

What do your attention and awareness look like when you are at Level 3?

_____

_____

_____

Emotional voice. Our emotional voice is separated, usually unsuccessfully, in a "not now" response. The voice isn't really quieted and will burst out if obstacles occur. Emotions are focused on feelings of stress and anxiety.

Write what your inner voice sounds like when you are at this level. (For example, my inner voice goes something like this: "Okay, okay, focus on getting this stupid task done. Gosh, I hate doing this! Okay, okay, get this done and hurry up! You're wasting time!" I'm not really thinking strategically. I'm just trying to urge myself into action.)

_____

_____

_____

Body engagement. We feel the fight-or-flight response, which is a physiological response to stress. Our heart rate increases, our adrenal gland releases cortisol (a stress hormone), and we receive a boost of adrenaline, which increases energy and anxiety. This fight-or-flight response occurs as we look for anything that may be a threat to us.

Where in your body do you feel your emotions the most when you are at Level 3? (For example, I tend to feel a tightening in my chest.)

ADHD symptoms. We use the fight-or-flight response as a coping mechanism to accomplish tasks. Because we are focused on a quick fix, we are trapped in repetitive and reactive patterns. Our short-term memory is even more unreliable.

What ADHD symptoms show up for you at Level 3? (For example, I hurry and make easily avoidable mistakes.)

Relation to others. Getting our own way is very important. We are quickly annoyed when people don't meet our expectations. We often look for what we can get from our relationships and aren't really concerned with giving back.

What do others experience when you are at this level? (For example, my family tells me that I give off a get-outta-my-way vibe.)

Level 4: Survival

Now let's move down the ladder. At Level 4, we are responsive to our greatest perceived threats. Our emotions start to take over to meet these threats. We begin to employ survival tactics—fight, flight, or freeze—as self-protective responses to our environment. We start to lose the ability to make reasonable choices and become fixated on the survival tactic we have chosen.

Think of a specific time when you were at Level 4 on the Emotional Health Ladder, and consider the questions below. If you can't recall enough information to answer, either ask a close friend or a family member or wait until you experience this level and then complete the questions.

Awareness and attention. Our awareness is reduced to looking for threats. We lack self-awareness and make decisions completely instinctively. Because of our focus on survival and getting our basic needs met, we indulge ourselves, physically and emotionally. We often do whatever we feel like doing—even when that isn't the healthiest option.

What do your attention and awareness look like when you are at Level 4?

Emotional voice. Our emotional voice is commandeering. It wants its emotional needs met immediately. Emotions are focused around feelings of fear and anxiety.

Write what your inner voice sounds like when you are at this level.

Body engagement. Our body remains on high alert; it eventually adapts and learns how to live with a higher stress level. We won't sleep as well, and we might gain or lose unhealthy amounts of weight.

Where in your body do you feel your emotions the most when you are at Level 4?

_____

_____

_____

_____

ADHD symptoms. Because we are constantly putting out fires, we find ourselves irritable, frustrated, and having poor concentration. Thinking tends to be mostly black-and-white at this stage.

What ADHD symptoms show up for you at Level 4?

_____

_____

_____

_____

Relation to others. We are self-centered and very critical of others and ourselves.

What do others experience when you are at this level?

_____

_____

_____

_____

Level 5: Delusional

At this level we are out of touch with reality. We are uncontrollable, unreasonable, and willing to destroy others and ourselves. Our mind obsessions completely take over our lives. Others may not see just how irrational we feel at this level, but we are certainly aware of it.

Think of a specific time when you were at Level 5 on the Emotional Health Ladder, and consider the questions below. If you can't recall enough information to answer, either ask a close friend or a family member or wait until you experience this level and then complete the questions. Some of my clients find this level difficult to discuss because it represents some of their worst instincts, but many find it useful to explore once they relax and become curious.

Awareness and attention. Our complete lack of awareness means that our behavior and decisions have the potential to be destructive to ourselves and others. Our attention to basic survival causes us to remain on the alert, constantly looking for threats to our emotional safety even though there may not be any.

What do your attention and awareness look like when you are at Level 5?

_____

_____

_____

_____

Emotional voice. Our emotional voice is fatigued but keeps screaming demands to have our emotional needs met. Intense emotions prevail in all situations. Fear, depression, and anxiety mark this level, resulting in exhaustion.

Write what your inner voice sounds like when you are at this level.

_____

_____

_____

_____

Body engagement. Struggling with stress for long periods has drained our physical, emotional, and mental resources to the point where our body no longer has the strength to fight stress. We may feel our situation is hopeless.

Where in your body do you feel your emotions the most when you are at Level 5?

_____

_____

_____

_____

ADHD symptoms. We are emotionally volatile, oversensitive, and oppositional.

What ADHD symptoms show up for you at Level 5?

_____

_____

_____

_____

Relation to others. We can be either very clingy or very distant and critical of others. We project our frustration and anger with ourselves onto others.

What do others experience when you are at this level?

_____

_____

_____

_____

Level 2: Attending To

Now let's move up the ladder. On Level 2, we are responsive to the most significant tasks without becoming emotionally overwhelmed or hitting snooze on our emotional voice. We have long periods of being present in a nonreactive moment. Emotions inform us rather than dominate us as we make decisions. We are more conscious of detracting moments and can keep them under control.

Think of a specific time when you were at Level 2 on the Emotional Health Ladder, and consider the questions below. If you can't recall enough information to answer, either ask a close friend or a family member, wait until you experience this level, or imagine how you would like to perform at this level.

Awareness and attention. We're often feeling good and managing our lives, even though we don't have the same degree of awareness as at Level 1. We are more attuned and open to ourselves and our environment.

What do your attention and awareness look like when you are at Level 2?

_____

_____

_____

_____

Emotional voice. Our emotional voice provides good information but isn't taking over by shouting. It informs our awareness.

Write what your inner voice sounds like when you are at this level.

_____

_____

_____

_____

Body engagement. Our breathing and posture both relax because we are not in a state of fight-or-flight.

Where in your body do you feel your emotions the most when you are at Level 2? (For example, I smile and laugh much more at this level.)

_____

_____

_____

_____

ADHD symptoms. Problematic symptoms are identified. Strategies and techniques are key to managing symptoms. They are used carefully and consistently.

What ADHD symptoms still show up for you at Level 2? How do you calmly accommodate them?

_____

_____

_____

_____

Relation to others. We look for win-win solutions.

What do others experience when you are at this level?

_____

_____

_____

_____

Level 1: Present and Calm

At this level, we are in a state of perpetual "presence." We have a quiet mind, and we are entirely in touch with the present moment, the now. We have behavioral freedom to respond to tasks, people, and situations the way we would like to respond.

Think of a specific time when you were at Level 1 on the Emotional Health Ladder, and consider the questions below. If you can't recall enough information to answer, either ask a close friend or a family member, wait until you experience this level, or imagine how you would like to perform at this level.

Awareness and attention. We respond as needed to whatever life presents, actualizing the positive potentials. We become more present and focused on what is actually happening around us. We are not fixated on defensive thoughts.

What do your attention and awareness look like when you are at Level 1?

_____

_____

_____

_____

Emotional voice. We are attuned to our emotions. Our emotional voice provides important guidance for us.

Write what your inner voice sounds like when you are at this level.

_____

_____

_____

_____

Body engagement. We feel more present and awake in our mind, heart, and body.

Where in your body do you feel your emotions the most when you are at Level 1?

_____

_____

_____

_____

ADHD symptoms. Symptoms are still present but are met with mindfulness, problem-solving, and planning.

What ADHD symptoms still show up for you at Level 1? How do you calmly accommodate them?

_____

_____

_____

_____

Relation to others. We respect and value relationships and regularly demonstrate this by our words and actions.

What do others experience when you are at this level?

_____

_____

_____

_____

REINFORCING
YOUR PERSONAL GROWTH

After examining how I move through the Emotional Health Ladder, I can see that

After examining how I move through the Emotional Health Ladder, I wonder if

After examining how I move through the Emotional Health Ladder, I decided that

After examining how I move through the Emotional Health Ladder, I am going to try to

BIG IDEAS
in Chapter 10

Healthy boundaries bring us
self-confidence and
self-respect and lead to higher
productivity, more energy,
and overall happiness.

11

Welcome Home

Creating Healthy Boundaries

The house-yard-fence analogy has helped many of my clients create more explicit boundaries for their thoughts and relationships. Using this analogy will help you think about the guidelines you have set for your life and identify areas where changes will increase your emotional health. Figure 8.1 at the back of the book can help in understanding the concepts discussed in the chapter.

REFLECTION on READING

After reading this chapter,

I felt _____ because _____

_____

_____

_____

I wondered why _____

_____

_____

_____

_____

I realized that _____

_____

_____

_____

_____

I decided that _____

_____

_____

_____

_____

Questions and Exercises

Before we dive into the house-yard-fence metaphor, let's first consider your core values, which serve as the foundation for setting boundaries. Taking this step will assist you in aligning your boundaries with what truly holds significance for you, thus ensuring that your interactions and relationships reflect your core beliefs and priorities. This clarity will make it easier for you to communicate and uphold boundaries effectively, resulting in healthier and more fulfilling connections with others.

Core Values

Look at the list of core values below, and circle the ten that most describe you. Then choose the top five from that list.

Having difficulty selecting the top five? Look at two of your values and ask yourself, "If I could satisfy only one of these, which would I choose?" It might help to visualize a situation in which you would have to make that choice. Keep working through the list, comparing each value with another value, until your list is in order.

Accountability	Diligence	Health	Results-oriented
Accuracy	Diversity	Helping society	Security
Achievement	Efficiency	Honesty	Self-actualization
Adventurousness	Empathy	Independence	Self-control
Altruism	Equality	Inner harmony	Selflessness
Ambition	Excellence	Intelligence	Self-reliance
Assertiveness	Excitement	Intuition	Serenity
Balance	Expertise	Joy	Service
Belonging	Exploration	Justice	Simplicity
Calmness	Expressiveness	Leadership	Spirituality
Carefulness	Fairness	Legacy	Spontaneity
Challenge	Faith	Love	Stability
Cheerfulness	Family	Loyalty	Strategy
Community	Fidelity	Making a difference	Strength
Compassion	Fitness	Mastery	Structure
Competitiveness	Fluency	Organization	Success
Consistency	Focus	Originality	Support
Contentment	Freedom	Positivity	Teamwork
Cooperation	Fun	Practicality	Thoroughness
Correctness	Generosity	Preparedness	Timeliness
Creativity	Goodness	Professionalism	Uniqueness
Curiosity	Grace	Prudence	Vision
Decisiveness	Gratitude	Quality-oriented	Vitality
Dependability	Growth	Reliability	Other: _____
Determination	Happiness	Resourcefulness	
Devoutness	Hard work	Restraint	

My top five values:

_____

_____

Explain how these values represent things you would support, even if your choice isn't popular and puts you in the minority. For example: You find yourself on a creative team that loves to brainstorm new ideas. You have a core value of practicality and believe that being pragmatic is essential for making informed decisions and achieving success. This means considering the facts and evidence when making decisions, rather than relying solely on emotions or intuition. You can see that some people on your team view your thinking as cold or unfeeling, but you continue to challenge them to make the most effective use of resources.

Assess how aligned your values are with your life. Do these values guide your words and actions, and if so, how?

_____

_____

_____

How do you feel when you make choices in line with your identified values versus times when you don't?

_____

_____

_____

What changes can you make in your life so that your choices and actions are more consistently in line with your values?

_____

_____

_____

The House-Yard-Fence Metaphor

Though boundary setting is difficult, it is vital for a healthy life. Taking responsibility for yourself by setting healthy perimeters is how you can increase your self-regulation and manage your ADHD.

THE HOUSE

Think of your internal self—your psyche and personhood—as a house. It's yours alone. No one is allowed to come in unless you have given them permission. It is an intimate space where no family members or close friends have the right to intrude.

Reflect on your house. What are some activities that make you feel most at home within yourself?

How do you create a safe space within your own mind?

Describe any particular people or experiences that have helped you build the foundation of your inner house.

How do you maintain the upkeep of your inner house, and what methods do you use to keep it strong and resilient?

In what ways do you allow yourself to be vulnerable within the walls of your inner house? How do you protect yourself from potential harm or negativity?

Reflect on troubling times you have endured. Identify times when you were scared. How did they affect your inner house?

Reflect on times when you felt alone. How did they affect your inner house?

Are there discarded, broken pieces of furniture representing sadness, envy, or regret scattered about your living room? Are there old boxes of resentment, guilt, or shame that need to be unpacked? Are there boxes filled with hurt, anger, fear, and anxiety cluttering the hallway?

Do you need help unpacking those boxes? Who is a safe person to enter your house to help you?

Physical boundaries. Everyone's boundaries in their house are unique. Setting boundaries with yourself is a way to maintain your house. The limits you create for yourself will reflect *your* values, needs, and priorities. What physical boundaries do you want to set for yourself?

Emotional boundaries. Setting emotional boundaries means recognizing your own emotional needs and taking steps to protect your mental health and well-being. It may involve limiting the amount of time you spend with someone who constantly vents negative emotions or clearly communicating your needs and expectations in a relationship. What emotional boundaries do you want to set for yourself?

Deep cleaning. What do you need to do to maintain your house? What repairs are needed? What is in the boxes cluttering your heart? Are they boxes of grudges, hurts, failures, shame, or envy?

When do you plan on cleaning out those boxes? What is the first step to begin that process?

Have you let someone or something into your house that doesn't belong there and needs to be evicted? What is the effect of having them there? What will you do?

Do you need help with this deep cleaning? Who could help you? Explain how you would tell someone about your "cleaning" goals. (For example: "I realize that I'm holding on to resentment about my childhood, and I want to learn how to get rid of it.")

THE YARD

Outside your house you have a yard. This is the space where special friends and loved ones gather. These are the folks you want to spend time with—people to whom you will send invitations for a grill-out and a party but who are not quite intimate enough to be allowed into your house. The people you invite into your yard are those you can trust to respect and appreciate this green space you have created and to help when you need it. When asked, they offer their opinions on plantings, maintenance, or the colorful gnomes you have placed around the yard. Yet they understand that they are only guests. They may offer opinions and suggestions, but ultimately it is your choice whether to accept their feedback.

Who is in your yard? Choose people to invite into this space whom you trust to care for you and who want to support you.

Once you have created a yard and invited trusted people to join you, you get to define your boundaries and be clear about what is acceptable and what isn't. To create great yard boundaries, you can clearly express the expectations you have for your guests and what good behavior looks like. These boundaries will include physical, emotional, mental, and spiritual parameters.

Have you ever rented a vacation home? Most of those places come with a nifty binder that welcomes you and explains the routines (like trash pickup) and rules (like no glass near the pool). With that in mind, write a letter to the individuals in your yard, extending a warm welcome and reiterating the routines and rules of your space. Reflect on your core values as you draft the letter, allowing them to serve as guiding principles. Although you never have to show anyone this letter, it will remind you of what is important to you and your yard.

THE FENCE

Fences help delineate where your yard begins and free access to you ends.

When you imagine your fence, what does it look like?

Do you have the right kind of fence? Can others identify it as a fence?

How do you know when you can let someone from the other side of the fence into your yard?

Write a letter to the people outside your fence. Greet them and remind them of your routines and rules. Reflect on your core values as you draft the letter, allowing them to serve as guiding principles. Although you never have to show anyone this letter, it will help you remember what is important.

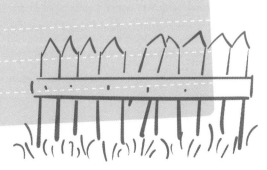

REINFORCING
YOUR PERSONAL GROWTH

What are the boundaries I want to create or protect?

How can I communicate my boundaries effectively and respectfully?

What are some practical steps I can take to set and maintain healthy emotional boundaries in my relationships and interactions?

Who or what could support me in making this change?

BIG IDEAS
in Chapter 11

12

Dancing through the Day

Hacks for Adulting

This chapter outlines three practical ways for individuals with ADHD to help themselves: managing sleep, protecting peak times, and learning to rehearse effectively.

REFLECTION on READING

Have you ever tried managing your sleep to help improve your ADHD symptoms? If not, why not? If so, what happened?

_____

_____

_____

How do you currently protect your peak times?

_____

_____

_____

In what ways do you think learning to rehearse effectively could benefit you in managing your ADHD?

_____

_____

_____

Is there a specific strategy from this chapter that you would be willing to try?

_____

_____

_____

Questions and Exercises

Managing Sleep

What is your relationship to the notion of sleep and going to bed?

1. I love sleep. I look forward to going to bed.
2. I conceptually understand that I need sleep and need to go to bed on time, but I get distracted and end up going to bed later than I want.
3. I don't believe that I need a lot of sleep.
4. I am like a night owl. I love staying up and being alone in my quiet house.
5. I think napping should be a national pastime.
6. It's just too difficult to try to go to sleep. I hate it.
7. Other: _____

Do you want to change your relationship with sleep? Why or why not?

_____

_____

_____

_____

> When you get enough sleep, you are more able to work efficiently during the day.

What do you need to do to get better sleep? Circle all that apply.

1. Plan my bedtime clearly and stick to it to ensure I get at least seven hours of sleep.
2. Focus on calming my mind and body for forty-five minutes before I expect to sleep.
3. Read about the importance of sleep.
4. Find time in my busy schedule to have alone time so I don't need to be a night owl.
5. Stop taking naps longer than twenty-five minutes during the day so I can sleep better at night.
6. Do relaxation exercises to calm down my body and brain.
7. See a professional to help me.
8. Other: _____

Are there any other techniques or strategies you have found helpful for managing your sleep with ADHD?

_____

_____

_____

_____

To improve my sleep, I will _____ and I will

_____ . I will also try _____ and _____

_____ .

Protecting Peak Times

Review your charts from pages 89–90 in chapter 7. What time of day (between 6:00 a.m. and 8:00 p.m.) do you do your best work—when you feel a high level of focus, attention, and efficiency?

_____

What tasks or activities can you do during that time frame that best use your high level of focus, attention, and efficiency?

_____

_____

_____

How do you know when you are in your peak times?

_____

_____

_____

How will you protect your peak times?

_____

_____

_____

Learning to Rehearse

Mental rehearsal is not positive self-talk or imagining scenes that make you feel good. Instead, it is carefully picturing yourself going through routines. When can you use the chair-flying technique discussed in this chapter (p. 169)?

_____

_____

_____

How can you remember to use this strategy?

_____

_____

_____

Have you ever used rehearsal in a negative way? What happened? How can you avoid doing this in the future?

_____

_____

_____

REINFORCING
YOUR PERSONAL GROWTH

While completing this chapter, I maintained a growth mindset by

I am proud of myself because

I decided to

BIG IDEAS
in Chapter 12

The most significant thing
you can do for your child is
to create a strong, healthy
relationship with them.

13

The Island of Misfit Toys

Parenting the ADHD Child

Raising emotionally healthy children who have ADHD is challenging. For a decade I have worked with families who are affected by ADHD. The children who do the best, who grow up to be the most emotionally healthy and resilient adults, have parents who have guided them in specific ways. These parents raise their children to have an authentic and healthy relationship with them. They teach their children the power of self-efficacy and resiliency. Children with ADHD can grow up to be confident adults if given the necessary nurturing and skills.

REFLECTION on READING

After reading this chapter,

I am feeling _____

_____

_____

_____

I am wondering _____

_____

_____

_____

I am wishing _____

_____

_____

_____

I want to learn more about _____

_____

_____

_____

I am frustrated that _____

_____

_____

_____

Questions and Exercises

Misfit Toys

When you were growing up, did you ever feel like a misfit toy? Describe what that felt like.

What are some specific memories you have of being a misfit toy?

What insight do these memories give you about parenting your children?

Describe your current relationship with your children. What do you want to improve?

In what ways are you showing endless empathy?

What can you do to improve demonstrating endless empathy?

Treating loved ones with dignity, affirming their worth, and respecting their boundaries and limitations are part of the modeling needed for children to develop respect for themselves and others. How are you modeling trusting respect in your family?

What can you do to improve trusting respect?

Stubborn love is a gift to a child with ADHD who feels like a misfit toy. How are you showing your stubborn love to your child?

What can you do to improve demonstrating stubborn love?

How do you practice gentle honesty in your family?

What can you do to improve demonstrating gentle honesty?

Self-Efficacy

Remember that you can teach your child to identify and challenge negative thoughts that undermine their belief in their ability to master a task, but the timing is important. Wait until they are calm and then challenge their negative thoughts.

What negative thoughts does your child have? When are good times to replace them with positive, truthful ideas?

_____

_____

_____

_____

How are you helping your child break down a task into small bits? What do you say when you give them praise for their progress on the small steps?

_____

_____

_____

It's important to give your child opportunities to control their environment, make decisions, use and practice their skills, and try different paths to achieve their goals. In what ways are you turning over the control of their environment to them?

_____

_____

_____

How are you contributing to your child's growth mindset? Are you modeling a growth mindset too?

_____

_____

_____

In what ways do you encourage your child to be a problem solver? Are you modeling problem-solving too?

Teaching your child about resiliency can help them bounce back from everyday stress and challenges. When they are resilient, they are braver, more curious, more adaptable, and more able to extend their reach into the world. In what ways are you lovingly encouraging their resilience?

Write a letter to your child telling them that you see their struggles and you are holding hope for them. Remind them of your love.

REINFORCING
YOUR PERSONAL GROWTH

What specific changes do I want to make?

What steps or actions have I thought about taking to initiate this change?

Who or what could support me in making this change?

BIG IDEAS
in Chapter 13

So many of my clients are
victors. They courageously
show up in their daily lives,
even when it isn't easy to do so.

14

Now What?

Writing Your ADHD Story

Let's examine your experience with ADHD using questions related to reorienting and recalibrating. Reorienting involves figuring out your current position, much like looking at a map to locate yourself. Recalibrating means making adjustments to your path to ensure you're headed in the right direction.

REFLECTION on READING

This book helped me understand that _____

_____

This book made me hope that _____

_____

This book made me wish that _____

_____

This book made me decide that _____

_____

This book made me look at _____

_____

This book made me believe that _____

_____

This book made me remember that _____

_____

This book made me wonder if _____

_____

This book made me want to_____

_____

Questions and Exercises

Reorient

Describe the messages you've picked up over the years from others about yourself or ADHD. Which ones are true?

_____

_____

_____

_____

What do you want people to know about you or your ADHD? How will you communicate that message to them?

_____

_____

_____

_____

Where do you want to take your ADHD story? What do you want to do with it?

_____

_____

_____

_____

Look through the Big Ideas that you gathered throughout your reading. What are your biggest takeaways?

_____

_____

_____

_____

_____

Was there a chapter that you found particularly useful? Why did it resonate with you?

_____

_____

_____

_____

Recalibrate

Recalibrating yourself means adjusting your course to make sure you are on the right track.

Write three ideas or strategies that you want to implement now.

_____

_____

_____

_____

_____

_____

Write your ideas or strategies on this chart:

Idea or Strategy	1	2	3
Why this idea or strategy is important to do now			
Steps I need to take to implement it			
Potential barriers			
How I can address potential barriers			
When I will check in to see how this idea or strategy is working (place reminder on calendar)			
Who can help me			
How I will keep using this idea or strategy			

REINFORCING
YOUR PERSONAL GROWTH

As I did these exercises, I demonstrated curiosity when I

As I did these exercises, I demonstrated courage when I

As I did these exercises, I demonstrated humility when I

As I did these exercises, I demonstrated honesty when I

As I did these exercises, I demonstrated a growth mindset when I

Dear Reader,

Congratulations! Your perseverance and remarkable determination have brought you to the finish line. I wish you the best, my friend, as you continue to grow in your understanding of yourself and how ADHD affects your life.

As I wrote this workbook, I imagined you diving into the exercises, conquering challenges, and navigating different ideas. I even imagined some of you arguing, telling me you wouldn't answer a specific prompt. I sincerely hope that completing this workbook didn't feel like mere pages but became an adventure in learning and self-discovery.

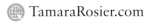

I'm genuinely interested in hearing about your experiences—what worked for you, what challenges you faced, and any feedback you might have. Your input is invaluable as I continue to create resources that resonate with and empower my wonderful readers. You can connect with me in the following ways:

🌐 TamaraRosier.com

📷 @Dr.TamaraRosier

in https://www.linkedin.com/in/tamara-rosier-phd

Thank you for completing this workbook. Your engagement means the world to me, and I'm excited to continue this journey of exploration and growth together. My book *You, Me, and Our ADHD Family* develops many of the topics introduced in this book. You can find it anywhere books are sold.

Keep growing,
Tamara

ADDITIONAL WORKSHEETS

Perceived Energy and Actual Energy

Our motivation is also affected by the amount of physical energy we *perceive* a task will require. We come to this conclusion by assigning each task a feeling, then through the lens of our hyperarousal, we gauge the difficulty of that task and how much energy it will use. As with our estimations of time, we tend to overestimate or underestimate the amount of energy we will need.

Create an awareness of your perceived energy versus actual energy. Try this activity:

1. Think about a task that you know you need to do but don't really want to do (e.g., answering an email, weeding the garden). What is your perceived energy to do this task? (1 = no energy/motivation, 10 = high energy/motivation) _____

2. Set your timer for ten minutes and begin the task. (I know you don't want to do it, but this is for science.)

3. When the timer goes off, mark your current energy. (1 = no energy/motivation, 10 = high energy/motivation) _____

4. Did your energy increase or decrease? If it increased, can you finish the task? If it decreased, what do you need to do to take care of your body (e.g., sleep, drink water)? Write your observations here:

_____

_____

_____

_____

Repeat this exercise so you can become aware of your *perceived* energy and your *actual* energy.

Perceived Energy and Actual Energy

Our motivation is also affected by the amount of physical energy we *perceive* a task will require. We come to this conclusion by assigning each task a feeling, then through the lens of our hyperarousal, we gauge the difficulty of that task and how much energy it will use. As with our estimations of time, we tend to overestimate or underestimate the amount of energy we will need.

Create an awareness of your perceived energy versus actual energy. Try this activity:

1. Think about a task that you know you need to do but don't really want to do (e.g., answering an email, weeding the garden). What is your perceived energy to do this task? (1 = no energy/motivation, 10 = high energy/motivation) _____

2. Set your timer for ten minutes and begin the task. (I know you don't want to do it, but this is for science.)

3. When the timer goes off, mark your current energy. (1 = no energy/motivation, 10 = high energy/motivation) _____

4. Did your energy increase or decrease? If it increased, can you finish the task? If it decreased, what do you need to do to take care of your body (e.g., sleep, drink water)? Write your observations here:

_____

_____

_____

_____

Repeat this exercise so you can become aware of your *perceived* energy and your *actual* energy.

Focus on the Yellow Quadrant

Many of us with ADHD have difficulty with the Yellow Quadrant. Try this exercise and increase your resilience in this quadrant.

Select a Yellow task that you need to accomplish today. Use the following questions to help you tackle this and other Yellow tasks.

Task: _____

What makes this a Yellow task for you?

_____

_____

_____

_____

Why does it need to be done?

_____

_____

_____

_____

When do you want to begin the task? (Block out the time on your calendar.)

_____

_____

_____

_____

Plan how you will accomplish this task. Be specific. Write a how-to list of the steps you need to take.

_____

_____

_____

_____

Look at your how-to list and plan how you will actually begin. Where will you work? What will you need around you?

_____

_____

_____

_____

How will you handle distractions and get back on track? What might be emotionally distracting to you while you work? How will you manage that? How will you guard yourself against malicious motivators?

_____

_____

_____

_____

_____

How will you know when you are finished? (This step helps you avoid the perfection trap.)

_____

_____

_____

_____

Set a timer for twenty minutes or less. Then begin the task.

1. When the timer alerts you, take a deep breath. How are you doing? What do you notice? (If you have hit a great rhythm with your task, congratulations! Keep going! If not, go to the next step.)

2. What is blocking you from completing this task? Check the box below.

   ☐ An emotional reason (e.g., you just hate this work so much that you don't want to do it)

   ☐ A technical reason (e.g., you don't have the information you need)

   ☐ A cognitive reason (e.g., you don't understand how to complete the task)

Explain why you checked the box you did.

_____

_____

_____

_____

If you have an *emotional reason*, try taking a short break and go to a timed Blue Quadrant activity. Attempt the task again after the break.

If you have a *technical reason*, write down what you need in order to complete the task. Rewrite your how-to list. Set the timer again.

If you have a *cognitive reason*, write down what you don't understand or know. How will you learn what you need to know? What resources could you use to fill in this gap? Rewrite your how-to list. Set the timer again.

Which strategy are you going to try?

_____

_____

_____

_____

Focus on the Yellow Quadrant

Many of us with ADHD have difficulty with the Yellow Quadrant. Try this exercise and increase your resilience in this quadrant.

Select a Yellow task that you need to accomplish today. Use the following questions to help you tackle this and other Yellow tasks.

Task: _____

What makes this a Yellow task for you?

_____

_____

_____

Why does it need to be done?

_____

_____

_____

When do you want to begin the task? (Block out the time on your calendar.)

_____

_____

_____

Plan how you will accomplish this task. Be specific. Write a how-to list of the steps you need to take.

_____

_____

_____

_____

Look at your how-to list and plan how you will actually begin. Where will you work? What will you need around you?

_____

_____

_____

How will you handle distractions and get back on track? What might be emotionally distracting to you while you work? How will you manage that? How will you guard yourself against malicious motivators?

_____

_____

_____

_____

How will you know when you are finished? (This step helps you avoid the perfection trap.)

_____

_____

_____

_____

Set a timer for twenty minutes or less. Then begin the task.

1. When the timer alerts you, take a deep breath. How are you doing? What do you notice? (If you have hit a great rhythm with your task, congratulations! Keep going! If not, go to the next step.)

2. What is blocking you from completing this task? Check the box below.

   ☐ An emotional reason (e.g., you just hate this work so much that you don't want to do it)

   ☐ A technical reason (e.g., you don't have the information you need)

   ☐ A cognitive reason (e.g., you don't understand how to complete the task)

Explain why you checked the box you did.

_____

_____

_____

If you have an *emotional reason*, try taking a short break and go to a timed Blue Quadrant activity. Attempt the task again after the break.

If you have a *technical reason*, write down what you need in order to complete the task. Rewrite your how-to list. Set the timer again.

If you have a *cognitive reason*, write down what you don't understand or know. How will you learn what you need to know? What resources could you use to fill in this gap? Rewrite your how-to list. Set the timer again.

Which strategy are you going to try?

_____

_____

_____

_____

NOTES

Introduction

1. See Carol S. Dweck, *Mindset* (New York: Ballantine Books, 2008).

Chapter 5 The Monsters We Face

1. Michel de Montaigne, *The Complete Essays of Montaigne*, trans. Donald M. Frame (Stanford, CA: Stanford University Press, 1976).

2. See T. E. Chansky, *Freeing Your Child from Anxiety: Powerful, Practical Solutions to Overcome Your Child's Fears, Worries, and Phobias*, 1st ed. (New York: Broadway Books, 2004).

TAMARA ROSIER, PhD, has been a college administrator, a professor, a leadership consultant, a high school teacher, a business owner, and an ADHD coach. Her multifaceted journey has equipped her with invaluable insights into ADHD and its impact on individuals' lives. As the visionary founder of the ADHD Center of West Michigan, Dr. Rosier spearheads a dedicated team comprising coaches, therapists, and speech pathologists. Together, they empower individuals, parents, and families with comprehensive understanding and practical skills to navigate  life with ADHD effectively. Dr. Rosier's books, *Your Brain's Not Broken* and *You, Me, and Our ADHD Family*, offer actionable strategies for addressing the profound emotional dimensions of ADHD.

Plutchik's Wheel of Emotion

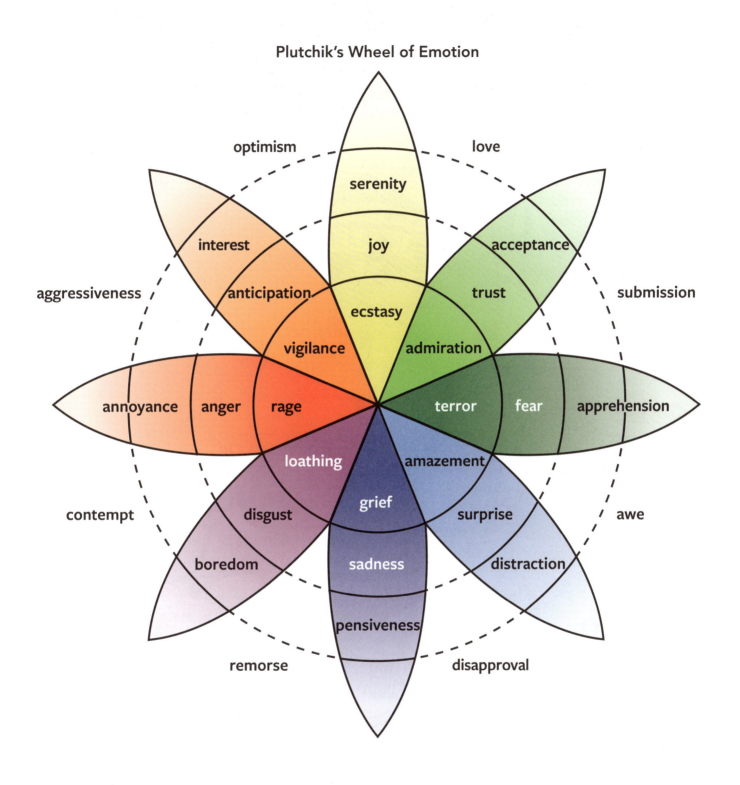

Figure 3.1

Figure 8.1

Figure 8.1

Figure 8.1

Figure 8.1

The Solve-It Grid

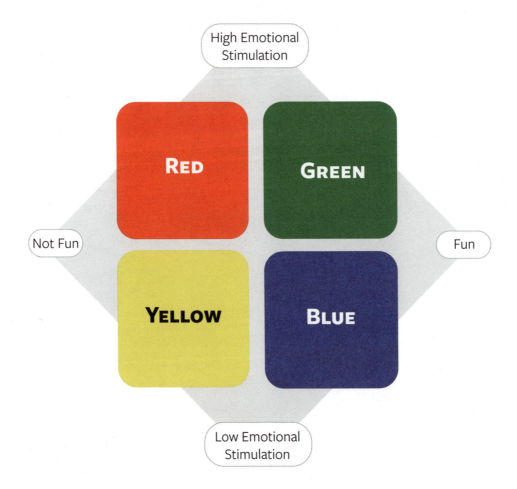

Figure 8.2